CAROLINA CURIOSITIES

Jerry Bledsoe's
Outlandish Guide
To the Dadblamedest Things
To See and Do
In North Carolina

The E...
Charlot...

Library of Congress Cataloging in Publication Data
Bledsoe, Jerry.
   Carolina curiosities.

   Includes index.
      1. North Carolina—Description and travel—
1981—   —Guide-books.   I. Title.
F252.3.B56   1984   917.56'0443   83-49042
ISBN 0-88742-007-9

Cover design by Raven
Typography by Carolina Compositors

East Woods Press Books
Fast & McMillan Publishers, Inc.
429 East Boulevard
Charlotte, North Carolina 28203

CONTENTS

The Piedmont (Cont.)

The Mountains 159

INTRODUCTION

I once knew a man who in his later years took to doing strange things.

He would, for example, stand on his head on top of his house, often for long periods. Or he would climb atop his house, get a running start and jump off. Once, he staged his own mock hanging.

If anybody asked why he did these things, his reply was always the same.

"Just for a dadblame cur'osity," he'd say with a big grin.

Well, that's precisely why I did this book. For a dadblame cur'osity. More precisely, for a lot of them, a whole heap, as we might say in North Carolina.

In nearly 20 years of roaming around North Carolina as a newspaper reporter and columnist, I've come upon a lot of cur'osities, dadblamed and otherwise, everything from natural wonders to esoteric little museums, oddball events, private fantasy worlds and North Carolina superlatives. Many of these things weren't widely known. They weren't in guidebooks. You couldn't pick up a travel brochure that would tell about them. No bumper stickers proclaimed them. No garish highway signs directed you to them.

It struck me that somebody ought to collect these curiosities into a guidebook so that people who have a taste for the offbeat could know about them.

Who better to do it than me, a person naturally drawn to such things?

In my travels and researches for this book, I'm sure that I didn't come upon nearly all the marvelous oddities that North Carolina has to offer. I know there must be wonders out there waiting to be discovered. If you know of any subjects worthy of inclusion in this book, I'd like to know about them for later editions. Write me at Route 6, Box 592, Asheboro, N.C. 27203.

THE
COASTAL PLAIN

BEAUFORT

AURORA

Fossil Museum

All of eastern North Carolina once lay deep under the ocean, and proof of it may be seen at Aurora's Fossil Museum.

Five miles north of Aurora, Texas Gulf operates a huge phosphate mine (phosphate is an essential ingredient of fertilizer), extracting from the earth minerals left behind by long-dead marine life. Fossils as old as five million years are often found in the huge pit, and some are on display at the museum, including giant teeth from 40-foot sharks, backbones from monstrous whales, bones from long extinct birds and skeletons of primitive dolphins that had necks, probably proof that they were land creatures that adapted to the sea.

But fossils aren't really the focus of the museum, which tries, through murals, slide shows, a simulated phosphate pit and other exhibits, to show how geological forces shaped the coastal area.

The museum is free. It's open Tuesday–Saturday, 10–5, in summer, by appointment the rest of the year. For more information, call Rusty Walker at (919) 322-5151.

BATH

Remains of Blackbeard's House

America's most famous pirate, Edward Teach, otherwise known as Blackbeard, came to Bath to take his 13th wife. He built a house across the creek from the village in 1712.

Six years later, Blackbeard's days of plunder were brought to an end in a shipboard battle with Lt. Robert Maynard, commander of a force sent by the governor of Virginia to capture him. Maynard is said to have sailed up the Pamlico River to Bath with Blackbeard's severed head displayed on the prow of his ship.

The remains of Blackbeard's house, which can be reached only by water, are on a point across the junction of Bath and Back creeks at the end of Bath's Main Street. Many believe Blackbeard buried gold in the area, but none has been found.

Blackbeard's exploits are celebrated in Bath each summer with an outdoor drama, *Blackbeard: Knight of the Black Flag,* in an amphitheater at Catnip Point (take the first left after entering the town). For more information call (919) 923-3971.

Mysterious Hoofprints

In a wooded area near the town of Bath is a series of saucer-size depressions in the earth that have mystified people for nearly 200 years. Nothing grows in the depressions, and debris placed in them will not remain.

Legend has it that the depressions were made by the hooves of a spirited horse ridden by a young man named Jesse Elliott in a race shortly after the turn of the 19th century. Local people frowned on Sunday horse racing, but Jesse and a group of other young men scorned them.

During one Sunday race, just after Jesse shouted, "Take me in a winner or take me to hell," his horse dug in its hooves, throwing Jesse into a nearby pine tree and killing him instantly.

The hoofprints are unmarked but regularly visited. To find them, take the Goose Creek State Park Road off U.S. Highway 264. The site is about a quarter mile on the left, near a pull-off created by the vehicles that stop there regularly.

North Carolina's Oldest Town and Church

Settled at the end of the 17th century, Bath became the first community in America to open a public library with the arrival of a shipment of religious books in 1700. In 1705, it became the first incorporated town in North Carolina. The following year, the first shipyard in the state was opened there, and the first public school soon followed. Bath became the state's first capital in 1744.

Some of the town's old buildings have been restored as a historic site and may be toured for a small fee. One building that is always open (no fee) is St. Thomas Episcopal Church, the state's oldest church, built in 1734 of brick shipped from England.

The church's treasured possessions include a 1704 Bible and candlesticks donated by King George II in 1740. The church bell, erected outside, was bought with funds given by Queen Anne and is 18 years older than the Liberty Bell.

For some reason, Bath never prospered and grew as some early seaport towns did. Some think it was because of George Whitfield's curse. Whitfield, a celebrated Methodist evangelist, came to Bath in 1774 to save souls. The townspeople not only wouldn't listen to him, they even refused him lodging. The Reverend Whitfield let them know just what he thought of their hospitality and religious views.

"I say to the village of Bath, village you shall remain, now and forever, forgotten by men and nations until such time as it pleases God to turn the light of His countenance again upon you."

Downtown Bath burned three times after the minister's visit, and the Reverend's curse was never forgotten.

For more information, call Bath Historic District at (919) 923-3971.

House Where Edna Ferber Researched
Her Most Famous Novel

The Palmer-Marsh house, built in 1744, is one of North Carolina's oldest houses. It was a rooming house when novelist Edna Ferber came to stay there in 1925, the year she won a Pulitzer Prize for her novel *So Big*. Ferber, who wrote panoramic novels about the American scene, came to research another novel.

In 1912, the James Adams Floating Theater, popularly called "The Showboat," was launched on a 128-foot-long barge in Washington, N.C., and was being towed to coastal communities by a 50-foot tugboat to bring musicals and comedies to entertainment-starved people in remote areas. Ferber stayed several weeks in Bath while observing and talking with the boat's crew and cast.

The novel she wrote from her experience, *Showboat*, appeared in 1926 and became a best seller. A play adapted from the book became a classic of American musical comedy and was made into a popular movie.

The John Adams Floating Theater burned in Savannah in 1941, and Ferber died in New York in 1968. The Palmer-Marsh house is now a museum, part of the Bath Historic District, and may be toured for a small fee.

Little mention is made of Ferber in Bath. She obviously didn't make a good impression. "She didn't leave a dime for the church," says local resident Ann Flanagan. "She complained about her lodging and she changed the locale of her novel to Mississippi, so she wasn't very popular here."

BELHAVEN

The Flea Wedding and Other Wonders
From Eva Way's Collections

Eva Way may have been the ultimate collector. Not only could Mrs. Way, a farm woman, not bear to throw anything away, she couldn't bear to see anybody else throw anything away either.

"Anybody who had anything they didn't want and didn't know what to do with, they took it to her," said her daughter, Catherine Wilkerson.

So Eva Way collected. Coins, shells, pitchers, books, magazines, newspapers, paintings, clothes, furniture, gourds, military paraphernalia, jewelry, radios, coffee mills, kitchenware, opium pipes, baskets, eyeglasses, pottery, typewriters, farm tools and even old everyday, worn-out shoes, which she prized above all other things. You name it, most likely Eva Way had a few, if not dozens of them.

It began with buttons when Mrs. Way was newly wed. She accumulated more than 30,000 different ones. She moved on to string from feed sacks, rolling it into huge balls. So compelling did her passion for collecting eventually become that she kept the freakish animals born on the farm, pickling them in jars and carefully labeling them ("hare-lipped puppy," "one-eyed pig"). Before it was over, she was even taking gallstones, cataracts, hideous ingrown toenails and tumors that doctors cut from her neighbors (one monstrous pickled tumor fills a 10-gallon aquarium).

Mrs. Way packed a 12-room house and a huge barn with her collections, and for more than 40 years she kept her home open to visitors who wanted to see it all. After her death at age 93 in 1962, her family was perplexed about what to do with everything.

"I tried to sell it all because I was sick and tired of it," said Mrs.

Wilkerson. "I sold for two years. After I got tired of selling, some ladies and I got together and decided to put it up as a museum."

The town of Belhaven accepted part of Mrs. Way's collections, and in 1965 the Belhaven Memorial Museum was opened on the second floor of the town hall.

The hit of the museum is Mrs. Way's dried flea wedding—all the fleas dressed and in church—which has to be viewed with a large magnifying glass. Nobody knows where Mrs. Way got it, but nobody was surprised that she had it.

The museum is free. It's open daily, 1-5. Group tours may be arranged by calling (919) 943-2381.

TERRA CEIA

Tulip Fields of Terra Ceia

In the '30s and early '40s of this century, a group of Dutch immigrants settled in the flat fields of Beaufort County. Lured by the rich, black soil, they came to grow the flowers of the old country: tulips, gladiolus, irises, daffodils, hyacinths, peonies, crocuses. At one time, 30 growers raised more than 500 acres of flowers. Now only one family remains a major grower, the Staalduinens, with 200 acres, mostly tulips. Several other families still grow a few acres, and in the spring and early summer, the fields around Terra Ceia blossom beautifully. The community is on State Road 1616, off U.S. Highway 264, near Pantego.

BERTIE

WINDSOR

The Largest Tree in North Carolina

A bald cypress two and a half miles northwest of Windsor on N.C. Highway 308 is the largest tree in the state, judging by a point system developed by the American Forestry Association.

The tree is 138 feet tall. The trunk has a circumference of more than 38 feet. The tree has 605 points, compared to 1,010 points for the largest tree in America, the General Sherman sequoia in California. Unfortunately, North Carolina's biggest tree isn't visible from the road and can be reached only by air or a two-mile round-trip hike through a swamp.

BLADEN

CARVERS

America's Largest Southern Magnolia

The nation's largest southern magnolia tree is on a farm owned by H. C. Blake at the end of State Road 1733, off N.C. Highway 87, east of Carvers. The tree stands 86 feet tall with a crown spread of 96 feet. The trunk has a circumference of 20 feet.

CLARKTON

Whistler's Mother's Homeplace

Part of an old brick chimney and the remains of a brick wall in a tangle of growth are the only traces left of stately Oak Forest, the plantation where James McNeill Whistler's mother, Anna, was born and reared.

Anna McNeill fell in love with a West Point classmate of her brother's, but the cadet, G. W. Whistler, married another woman. After seven years of marriage and three children, Whistler's wife died and he renewed his romance with Anna. They married when she was 27, and Anna gave birth to five sons. Her first-born, James, nicknamed Jamey, would become a painter and make his mother famous.

After G. W. Whistler, an engineer, took a job building a railroad in Russia, tragedy befell the family. Anna, who had followed her husband abroad, lost him and three of her sons to illness and returned to this country.

For a while during the Civil War, she lived at Oak Forest, but her uneasiness at being the widow of a West Point man prompted her to move to safety in Paris. It was there that her son James visited her and painted her portrait. He called it "Arrangements on Gray and Black," but it became known as "Whistler's Mother." Owned by the French government, it is on permanent exhibit at the Louvre in Paris.

Anna McNeill Whistler died in 1881 at age 77 and is buried in England. Oak Forest, built in 1737, burned in 1933. The remains are just north of Clarkton on an unpaved road, a half mile off State Road 1760, 1/10 of a mile from U.S. Highway 701.

BRUNSWICK

CALABASH

Seafood Restaurant Town

Calabash, a one-time fishing village named for an Indian word for gourds, is a town of just over 200 people with a seafood restaurant for every ten residents.

Just who opened the first restaurant in town, the Becks or Colemans, is a matter of dispute. Both families were holding outdoor oyster roasts for people from nearby communities back in the '30s. By 1940, both had moved their oyster roasts indoors and added fried seafoods.

As more customers came to eat with the Becks and Colemans, other restaurants, or fish camps, as they came to be called in North Carolina, opened in the small community, and by the '60s Calabash was drawing large crowds from nearby, ever-burgeoning Myrtle Beach.

By the '70s, Calabash had attracted national attention and Calabash-style cooking, meaning lightly battered seafood briefly fried, was being advertised by restaurants over several Southern states.

Once Calabash restaurants featured fresh seafood locally caught, but now most of it is caught elsewhere and frozen. Newer restaurants not only brought gaudy signs, bright lights and salad bars but also fancy dishes like lobster to Calabash's simple fare, changing the whole character of Calabash.

Calabash's restaurants are lined side-by-side on N.C. Highway 179, just off U.S. Highway 17, near the South Carolina line, and along a side street leading to the waterfront. Both original restaurants, Beck's and the Coleman's Original Calabash, are still operated by their families.

In the '40s, a frequent diner at the Colemans' restaurant was entertainer Jimmy Durante. Lucy Coleman remembers that he joked with her and called her Mrs. Calabash. Durante later began closing all of his shows by saying, "Goodnight, Mrs. Calabash, wherever you are," and Lucy Coleman believes he was talking to her.

SHALLOTTE

North Carolina's Only Nudist Subdivision

The Apollo Sun Club, founded in 1976 by New England transplants Harry and Jackie Cohenno, is North Carolina's only nudist resort and community.

Affiliated with the American Sunbathing Association, the club includes Bare Lake; tennis, shuffleboard and volleyball courts; a hot tub, whirlpool and sauna; a clubhouse and other recreational facilities, plus leased lots for mobile homes and rental lots for campers. Building lots are for sale in the adjoining Vinwood and Forest Grove nudist subdivisions.

Clothing is not allowed in recreational areas in daylight when the temperature is over 76 degrees and raining or over 68 degrees and clear and never in the lake, sauna, hot tub and shower area.

Events are held at the resort year-round, and visitors are allowed three visits before they must become members.

The resort, only 14 miles from North Myrtle Beach, S.C., is two miles off U.S. Highway 17, one mile from N.C. Highway 904, on State Road 1315. Visitors should make advance arrangements. Write Harry Cohenno, P.O. Box 936, Shallotte, N.C. 28459, or call (919) 287-6404.

CARTERET

BEAUFORT

Captain Sinbad's Pirate Cruises, Pirate School and Pirate Invasion

When Ross Morphew was growing up in Ohio, the only thing he wanted to be was a pirate. When people told him that wasn't possible, he asked why. So when he grew up, he built himself a brigantine in his back yard and eventually set sail for the North Carolina waters once plied by the famous pirate Blackbeard. He outfitted his ship with cannon, flew the Jolly Roger, donned pirate garb, changed his name to Capt. Sinbad, and began attacking vessels with water balloons and occasionally spiriting away willing fair maidens.

He began taking passengers for short cruises on his ship, the Meka II, and in 1979 he opened the world's first pirate school, offering five-day cruising courses in such skills as burying treasure, plank walking, swinging from the yardarms, yo-ho-hoing and swashbuckling.

Each year on the fourth weekend in April, Captain Sinbad and a band of rogues invade Beaufort and try to take it over. Each year they are beaten back by a hardy band of defenders with musketry and cannon.

For more information, call (919) 728-7123.

Strange Seafood Exhibition

Ever tried marinated octopus? How about raw squid? Live sea urchin eggs? Charcoaled shark? Mole crab soup? Smoked eel? Seaweed salad? Stingray casserole? Left-handed whelk chowder?

Thousands of people have tried such exotic fare at the Hampton Mariners Museum's annual Strange Seafood Exhibition, held on the third Thursday of August. The event, designed to show that many strange creatures from sea and sound are not only edible but quite good (a few are pretty awful, too), features more than 50 different dishes prepared by local cooks. Demonstrations show how to gather, catch, open, clean and prepare various creatures for eating.

This has become one of the most popular events on the North Carolina coast, attracting national attention every year. It grew to such a degree that crowds were no longer manageable, and now participation is limited to 1,000 people. A fee is charged and tickets should be ordered early.

For more information, write Judith Spitsbergen, Hampton Mariners Museum, 120 Turner Street, Beaufort, N.C. 28516, or call (919) 728-7317.

MOREHEAD CITY

Blue Crab Derby

How fast can a crab run? You can find out at the Blue Crab Derby held each year in front of the N.C. Marine Fisheries building on U.S. Highway 70 West in Morehead City.

Races are held for both amateur and professional crab trainers, but few professionals show up because Jean Paul Lewis, a crabber from Smyrna and all-time champion speed crab trainer, almost always wins all the trophies in the professional division.

In addition to the races, musical entertainment is provided along with crab dinners. You can choose crab cakes or steamed crabs for dinner, and don't be surprised if you think you see some of the racers on your plate.

"We eat all the losers," says Bill Colbert, a member of the Kiwanis Club which sponsors the event. Call him for more information at (919) 726-2516.

Old Quawk's Day

He was a cantankerous old salt, irritable and irreligious, who washed ashore from a shipwreck in the last century and stayed. Other fishermen couldn't pronounce his name, so they called him Old Quawk, because his squawking voice resembled the call of the night heron, more commonly called the quawk.

One blustery March day when threatening skies kept other fishermen in port, Old Quawk cursed the heavens, went to retrieve his nets—and disappeared into legend.

Old Quawk Day is held the second Saturday in March at the Morehead Municipal Park on U.S. Highway 70 West to honor the memory of the legend.

Events include a quawk-calling contest, an Old Quawk look-alike contest, scallop skipping and flounder flinging. Scallop skippers compete to see how many times they can make a scallop bounce on the waters of Bogue Sound. Flounder flingers see how far they can throw a slimy dead flounder.

Miserable weather is preferred for the event, but it is held even in pleasant conditions. For information call Carteret County Chamber of Commerce at (919) 726-6831.

Bald-Headed Men of America
Headquarters and Convention

Don't pretend to shield your eyes from the glare of John Capps's shiny head. Don't ask him if flies trying to land on his head skid and break their legs. They're old jokes. Call him Curly if you like, but don't expect him to laugh.

Do expect him to use a lot of lines on you.

"My philosophy is: If you haven't got it, flaunt it."

"The Lord is just, the Lord is fair, he gave some brains, the others hair."

"I'm just trying to set a shining example."

John started losing his hair at age 15. By 20, he was bald. "I'm the fourth generation of baldness in my family," he says. "I grew up in a family where baldness was accepted, a way of life, so to speak. It didn't bother me at all."

But he knew it bothered a lot of other people, and that set him to thinking. In 1974, when he was 33, living in Dunn, John started Bald-Headed Men of America to promote pride in baldness. It wasn't an idea

John Capps setting a shining example

that came off the top of his head. He thought about it for a long time.

The organization stirred international attention and attracted nearly 10,000 members, including celebrities such as Yul Brynner, Telly Savalas and former President Gerald Ford. John, who became a celebrity himself, constantly in demand for appearances, moved his organization to Morehead City because he thought it a more appropriate location.

"More head, less hair," he says.

At the group's headquarters in his print shop on Arendell Street (U.S. Highway 70 West), John offers Bald Is Beautiful bumper stickers and gag gifts such as toothless combs. On the second Saturday in September each year, he holds a convention at Mrs. Willis's Restaurant where baldies compete for such titles as sexiest, smoothest, prettiest and most kissable bald heads.

For more information, write Bald-Headed Men of America, Arendell Street, Morehead City, N.C. 28577, or call (919) 726-1004.

NEWPORT

World's Largest Pig Picking

In 1979, the Newport Development Center for children faced a crisis because of federal and state budget cuts. A group of citizens decided to hold a pig cooking contest to try to keep the center operating.

They got 25 sponsors, 25 cooks and 25 pigs and hoped to sell 2,500 plates of barbecue. Days before the event, they realized they'd sold too many tickets and had to scramble to get 17 more pigs, cooks and sponsors.

Now 100 pigs are cooked every year on the first weekend in April, the biggest pig cooking contest anywhere. The competition is keen and the judging is harsh (the pigs, which cook all night, are judged on appearance, color, crispness of skin, doneness, taste, moisture and sauce).

Thousands of people come to eat the results and see the entertainment, which includes music, dancing and peripheral contests (in 1983, a Marine choked to death before hundreds of people during a doughnut eating contest at the event). For more information, call (919) 223-4304.

SEALEVEL

Snug Harbor Day

Capt. Richard Randall, a privateer in the early days of this nation's history, made a lot of money from the sea and in his will, penned by his friend Alexander Hamilton, he left money to build a home where "aged, decrepid and worn-out seamen" could spend their final days. He decreed that it be called Sailors Snug Harbor.

The home was built on Staten Island in 1801 and there it remained, overseen by trustees, until 1976 when deteriorating buildings forced a move. Seeking a less crowded area in a milder climate to build a new home, the trustees settled on a site on Nelson's Bay at Sealevel, near the eastern end of U.S. Highway 70. More than 100 old mariners make their homes at Sailor's Snug Harbor, about a tenth of them female.

Snug Harbor Day was begun as a means of acquainting the old seafarers with the community. Arts and crafts are displayed. Food is served along with music, dancing and other entertainment. But the greatest entertainment is listening to the residents of Snug Harbor tell sea stories.

The event is held each year in spring, but no particular day is set. For more information, call the home at (919) 225-4411.

CHOWAN

EDENTON

America's Largest Sand Post Oak

The largest sand post oak tree in America stands in the front yard of

Herbert Wilson's house on N.C. Highway 32 north of Edenton, next to the N.C. Forest Service headquarters and fire tower. The tree is 70 feet tall with a crown spread of 79 feet. The trunk has a circumference of 11 feet.

Oldest Frame House in North Carolina

In 1972, Dr. Richard Hines, Jr., a dentist, bought an old frame house on the Yeopim River that once had been in the family of his wife, Ann. The following year, he moved it to Horni Blow Point on Albemarle Sound to a lot on Bella Vista Drive, off N.C. Highway 37. He added to it a den, two bedrooms, a laundry and bath and made it into a home for his family.

Documents indicate that the house, which once was called Pine Grove and later Sycamore, may have been built in 1718, perhaps by Jacob Butler, thus making it the oldest standing frame house in North Carolina. Controversy exists about this, however. Some maintain that the Cupola House, a visitors center on Broad Street in Edenton, built around 1725, is the oldest.

Peanut Festival

Peanuts are very big in Edenton, both literally and figuratively. Some of the biggest peanuts in the world are grown near the town (it's the home of Jimbo's Jumbos), and peanuts are also the town's major industry.

Of the 15,000 acres of cropland in Chowan County, more than 6,000 are planted in peanuts, and Edenton has three major peanut processing plants. So it was only natural that the town start a Peanut Festival, which it did in 1976.

Held the first weekend in October to celebrate the harvest, the festival features a peanut parade, peanut picking demonstrations, peanut rolling races (you roll 'em with your nose) and other events. Plenty of peanuts are available for eating raw, roasted, fried or made into peanut brittle—but you won't find any boiled, the way peanuts are best prepared for eating.

"People in this area don't eat boiled peanuts very much for some reason," says Betty Cox, who helps organize the event. Call her for more information at (919) 482-8431.

COLUMBUS

CHADBOURN

Oldest Fruit Festival in the South

Chadbourn once called itself the strawberry capital of the world. From the turn of the century to the mid-thirties, strawberries were the major crop in the area.

Millions of quarts of strawberries were shipped out of Chadbourn in refrigerated railroad cars each year. Once, a million quarts were shipped in a single 24-hour period. When a problem developed one year with railroad cars, tons of strawberries soured and had to be dumped in a nearby swamp. Old-timers remember that the water ran red for days.

The strawberry auction, which brought hundreds of growers and buyers to town each spring, was the highlight of the year in Chadbourn, and the Strawberry Festival, begun in 1932, grew out of it.

The auction is no more, but the festival has continued each year, making it the oldest agricultural festival in the state, and one of the oldest in the country, although soybeans and tobacco long ago replaced strawberries as area farmers' big money producers. Indeed, only a few farmers grow about 125 acres of strawberries in the area now, mostly for local sale.

But Chadbourn still holds the Strawberry Festival each year on the first Friday in May out of tradition. A parade is held, along with a strawberry recipe contest. Fresh strawberries and strawberry short-cake are sold on the streets. And farmers bring their biggest and sweetest strawberries to be judged in 24 divisions.

The winning 6-quart flats of strawberries are then sold at a charity auction. Take a lot of money if you plan to buy any. Most go for about $200 a flat, and some have brought as much as $1,200. For more information, call Richard Tyler at (919) 654-3408.

LAKE WACCAMAW

South's Largest Crater Lake

Lake Waccamaw, a shallow black-water lake five miles long and three miles wide, named for local Indians, is the largest of the Carolina Bays, a widely spread series of oval-shaped lakes, swamps, peat beds and depressions in southeastern North Carolina. The bays are believed to have been caused by a meteor shower striking the earth thousands of years ago.

The lake is drained by the Waccamaw River, a beautiful, twisting stream greatly favored by canoeists. The northern edge of the lake can be reached by N.C. Highway 214 from the town of Lake Waccamaw on U.S. Highway 74-76.

Lakes White, Bay Tree and Singletary in Bladen County are also Carolina Bays.

WHITEVILLE

Grave of World's Second-Most Famous Siamese Twins

On July 11, 1851, twin girls joined at the hip were born to slaves Jacob and Monemia on Jabe McCoy's plantation in the Welches Creek community northeast of Whiteville.

At that time, the original Siamese twins, Chang and Eng, who had gained worldwide fame exhibiting themselves, had settled in western North Carolina, where they married sisters and were rearing families.

McCoy was quick to realize the possibilities for his twins and sold them before they were a year old for $1,000 and 25 percent of the income from exhibiting them. But the buyer had little success showing them so young, and when they were 2, McCoy waived all rights to them for $200.

The twins were sold again and by the age of 4 were being exhibited in Europe, where doctors determined their spines were fused, making separation impossible.

Although they had clearly separate nervous systems and minds of their own, the twins, named Mille and Christine at birth, called themselves Mille-Chrissy, thought of themselves in the singular, and frequently walked on only two of their four legs. Extraordinarily congenial, they learned to recite and sing sweetly at their exhibitions.

By age 10, the twins were back in this country, and the owner who had inherited them, Joseph Pearson Smith of South Carolina, hid them near Spartanburg during the Civil War to keep them out of the hands of Union troops.

After winning their freedom following the war, the twins, who were exceptionally bright, hired a manager and again toured Europe, where they gained great fame for their singing, learned to speak fluently in five languages, and became special favorites of England's Queen Victoria, who frequently summoned them to perform.

By the turn of the century, the twins had returned to their birthplace and built a 14-room house on property once owned by the man who had owned them at birth. There they frequently received friends and family and entertained on the big front porch. But in 1909 the house burned, destroying all the mementoes of their world travels.

Soon after the fire, Mille contracted tuberculosis and grew steadily weaker. She died peacefully on the afternoon of October 8, 1912, at age 61, in the presence of Dr. W. H. Crowell of Whiteville, who had made acquaintance with the twins while studying in England. Chrissy, who detected her sister's death before the doctor, lived less than a day (reports vary from 8 to 17 hours) and spent her last hours calmly praying and singing favorite hymns.

The twins were buried in a double cypress coffin in the cemetery of a small Baptist church near their home. A metal grave marker was melted in a forest fire that swept through the area years later.

In 1969, the Columbus County Historical Society got family permission to move and remark the grave. The remains were reburied in the Welches Creek Community Cemetery not far from the original site and a granite marker was erected. "A soul with two hearts," reads part of the inscription. "Two hearts that beat as one."

The Welches Creek Cemetery is on State Road 1719, off Red Hill Road, off U.S. Highway 74-76, east of Whiteville.

CRAVEN

CROATAN

Tom Haywood's Self-Kicking Machine

Tom Haywood opened a country store in 1919 and became a prominent man, a county commissioner. The story is that one day in 1937 Tom did something that made him want to kick himself, and unable to do the job

Tom Haywood's self-kicking machine

to his satisfaction, he got his friend Wilber Herring to build him a kicking machine.

Wilber came up with a machine with four old shoes on metal spokes, a hand crank and belt drive. Tom put it under a shed near his store and erected a big sign proclaiming it to be "Home Office, the Self-Kicking Club."

That's the story. The reality is that Tom was a man who liked to have fun and knew how to attract attention. His kicking machine drew a lot of attention. It was featured in Universal News Reel, on the CBS radio show "We the People," in newspapers and magazines worldwide.

Tom Haywood died in 1955. His store on U.S. Highway 70 is now owned by Dino and Donna Vignanpiano, formerly of New York, and his kicking machine still attracts media attention and draws hundreds of visitors each year.

NEW BERN

The Great Trent River Raft Race

The strangest things come floating past New Bern's Bicentennial Park each year on the second Saturday in June.

Floating pickup trucks, crude pirate ships, ladders riding on inner tubes, and one year even a 40-foot, fire-breathing dragon. Nobody knows what's coming next. But each year more than 30,000 people turn out to watch as a strange flotilla of homemade craft carrying more than 500 would-be sailors compete for trophies.

The races, sponsored by radio station WAZZ, have been held since 1976 to aid the Shriners Burn and Crippled Children Hospitals. Bicentennial Park is at Union Point, where the Neuse and Trent rivers meet, near downtown New Bern. For more information call Bill Poole at (919) 637-6144.

Hall of Fame Cypress

In the walled back yard of the Samuel Smallwood Myers House (built in 1884), a private residence, is North Carolina's most famous tree. Thought to be more than 1,000 years old, it's one of 20 trees in the Hall of Fame of American Trees. Early settlers signed a peace treaty with

Indians under the tree, and both George Washington and James Monroe visited the tree. It can be seen from a public alley beside the house by climbing onto a car fender and peeking over the wall.

Swiss Bear Festival

New Bern, settled in 1710 by Swiss immigrants, took its name from Bern, Switzerland, and each year it celebrates that heritage with a street festival on the second weekend in October.

It's called the Swiss Bear Festival because of the famous bear pits in Bern, but no bears are present for New Bern's celebration. Instead, there are beer gardens, German beer bands, street dancing, antique and crafts shows. A Coast Guard cutter is open for tours, and Tryon Palace, North Carolina's first capitol, opens its grounds and formal gardens with its spectacular chrysanthemum displays for free. For more information, call Swiss Bear, Inc., (919) 638-5781.

Fred the Stuffed Fire Horse

Back in the days when fire engines were run by steam and pulled by horse, Fred was one of New Bern's most dependable fire horses. The town had two volunteer fire companies, Atlantic, organized in 1845, and Button, organized 20 years later. Fred became a fire horse in 1908 and pulled a hose wagon for Atlantic Company.

Fred always knew just what to do when the alarm sounded, always responded quickly, backing into the wagon stall so the harness could be dropped over his head. He always ran hard and seemed to take pride in getting his hose to fire scenes as quickly as possible. He must have sensed that his working days were numbered, though, after the town got its first motorized fire wagon in 1914. Another followed a year later.

But that didn't stop Fred from giving his all. He strived to beat the chugging trucks at every opportunity.

Fred helped fight the biggest fire that New Bern has ever seen, a holocaust that struck in December, 1922, and nearly burned down the town. It destroyed churches, stores, warehouses, a shipyard and more than 1,000 houses. A hundred buildings were dynamited to try to stop its spread. More than 3,200 people were left homeless.

Maybe it was memories of that awful fire, or maybe it was just the ever-growing threat from the newfangled fire engines that caused Fred to strain ever harder at the sound of the alarm. Whatever it was, the strain proved too great.

In 1925, while racing to an alarm from old box 57 at New Banks and North streets, Fred fell dead in his harness. The alarm proved false.

Because of Fred's noble efforts, the men of Atlantic Company decided to have his head stuffed. They kept it at the fire station until 1957 when the town opened its Firemen's Museum in an old garage behind the fire station.

The museum, one of a few of its kind in the world, contains New Bern's old fire engines and wagons and a great assortment of other firefighting paraphernalia and memorabilia, but Fred's stuffed head has always been its featured attraction. The museum is now in a new building on Hancock Street, just around the corner from the fire station.

Birthplace of Pepsi-Cola

Caleb Bradham was called Doc because he liked to mix remedies in his pharmacy at the corner of Pollack and Middle streets. He made tonics for rheumatism, cramps, coughs, dandruff, constipation and dog mange. But it wasn't until he concocted a new soft drink to sell at his marble-topped fountain that he finally hit on something that would make him rich.

All of his customers liked his new drink, which they called Brad's Drink. That gave Bradham the idea that he should turn over his drugstore to an assistant and hit the road selling the syrup he used to make his drink. He didn't particularly like calling it Brad's Drink, so for $100 he bought a registered brand name, Pep Kola, from a defunct New Jersey company, and changed it to Pepsi-Cola, which he thought had more bounce. Within ten years, Bradham's drink was being sold in 24 states, and he was a rich man.

After World War I, problems arose. The price of sugar shot up dramatically, and fearing a shortage, Bradham invested heavily in it. Soon the market broke and the price of sugar fell to a fourth of what it had been. It broke Bradham and his company closed. He returned to his drugstore and his remedies.

Pepsi-Cola might have disappeared completely if a few distributors hadn't stockpiled barrels of syrup. The formula for making Pepsi and the registered name had been bought from receivership, sold and resold before another company started making the drink in the '30s, a few years after Bradham's death.

Pepsi went on to become America's second most popular soft drink (after Coca-Cola), but Bradham's family never received any of the riches it produced.

The pharmacy where Bradham invented Pepsi is now Hearnes'

Jewelry Store. A plaque on an outside wall identifies it as the birthplace of the famous drink. If he isn't busy, jeweler Richard Hearnes will take visitors to see the spot in the basement where Bradham actually mixed the first batch of syrup.

CUMBERLAND

FAYETTEVILLE

Site of Babe Ruth's First Home Run

The year was 1914. The Baltimore Orioles had come to Fayetteville for three weeks of spring training that March because Hyman Fleishman, a transplanted Baltimorean, offered them free lodging at his Lafayette Hotel.

Joining the Orioles that year was a new player, 18-year-old George Herman Ruth. Because he was cherub-faced and the youngest member of the team, the other players started calling him Babe.

During an intra-squad game at the old Cape Fear Fairgrounds off Gillespie Street, "the babe" hit a ball 405 feet out of the park, across a corn field and into a lake, his first, unofficial home run as a professional player. He later would go on to hit 714 official home runs in his career, a record broken only by Hank Aaron.

The ballpark is gone now. A State Highway Department office occupies the site. But a historic marker has been erected by the state, thanks to a three-year campaign by Maurice Fleishman, son of Hyman, who as a bat boy for the Orioles saw Babe hit that first home run.

House Where Carson McCullers Wrote Her First Novel

Carson McCullers, a Georgia native who became one of the South's most highly acclaimed writers, lived with her husband, Reeves, on the second floor of Cool Spring Tavern at 119 Cool Spring Street from 1938 to 1940, while she was finishing her first novel, *The Heart Is a Lonely Hunter.*

The couple moved to Fayetteville because Reeves was transferred there by the loan company he worked for, and they disliked the town intensely. McCullers' book was published to rave reviews in 1940, and the couple used the first royalties to move to New York. A Peeping Tom incident that occurred at Ft. Bragg while McCullers was living in Fayetteville inspired her second novel, *Reflections in a Golden Eye.*

Tenth Hole of Original Putt Putt

Don Clayton, a former quarterback at the University of North Carolina, was a hot shot insurance agent in his hometown, making a lot of money and sometimes working 20 hours a day, when he realized something was wrong. His doctor told him he was about to have a nervous breakdown and advised him to take a month off.

During that month, Don played a round of miniature golf at a crude course and was struck by the idea that the game would be more fun on a better designed, more challenging course. So he sat down and designed one he thought would be better. He built it for $2,500 on leased land on Bragg Boulevard at a junction called the Crossover, and opened it on June 21, 1954.

He was planning to call the place Shady Vale Miniature Golf Course, but when he went to open an account at the bank, he realized he wasn't sure how to spell Vale and began trying to think of another name.

"I said, 'Well, it's putting,'" he recalls, "'and what rhymes with putt?' There wasn't anything, so I called it Putt Putt."

His golf course was an immediate success and by that fall he had already started building others in other cities. There are now more than 1,400 Putt Putts around the world, all of them using the holes, green carpets and orange rails designed by Don.

The original Putt Putt is gone. The lease on the land expired after 14 years and Don built a new 54-hole course two blocks west on Bragg Boulevard. But the concrete part of the tenth hole of the original course still exists behind the One-Hour Koretizing Dry Cleaners and Kasey's Restaurant.

FT. BRAGG

War Games

Ft. Bragg, one of America's largest military bases, home of the 82nd Airborne, the First Special Operations Command and the 18th Airborne Corps, America's premier ready force, is an open post allowing free access to visitors.

Parachute drops are made almost daily at the sprawling post, and visitors are invited to watch. Time of the jumps and locations of drop zones are recorded daily on tapes at the visitors center at the Main Post Parade Field on Randolph Street.

Two more interesting spots for visitors are the 82nd Airborne Museum, where the story of the 82nd is told in a slide show, and a large amount of memorabilia, especially from World War II, including captured weapons and materiel, airplanes that paratroopers jumped from and a mock-up of a World War II glider may be seen.

Weapons and paraphernalia from the Vietnam War may be seen at the Special Forces Museum, which features a mock-up of a Special Forces raid in Vietnam.

Both museums are on Ardennes Road, about three miles apart.

Groups may arrange demonstrations of scout dog and Special Forces training by calling (919) 396-5407. Ft. Bragg is on Fayetteville's western edge, accessible by N.C. Highways 24, 87 and 210.

DARE

BUXTON

Tallest Lighthouse in America

Cape Hatteras Lighthouse, built of brick in 1870, is 208 feet tall, making it the tallest lighthouse in the United States. Its automatic light, warning ships of the most treacherous waters of the Atlantic Coast, can be seen 51 miles off shore. Visitors may climb the 268 steps of the lighthouse to get a panoramic view of Hatteras Island.

The lighthouse is threatened by the ever-encroaching surf, and a campaign has been started to raise money to keep it from being claimed by the waters it warns against.

The lighthouse, just south of Buxton, off N.C. Highway 12, is maintained by the National Park Service.

Hatteras lighthouse, tallest in America

HATTERAS

First National Seashore

In 1833, Frank Stick, an artist, wrote an article suggesting that much of North Carolina's Outer Banks—fragile, largely wild barrier islands that he had chosen for his home—should be preserved as a coastal park. The idea caught on and such a park was authorized by Congress in 1937.

View from America's tallest lighthouse

World War II intervened before the park could be established, however, and for a while the plan seemed dead. But it was revived after the war and land acquisition began. Dedicated finally in 1958, Cape Hatteras National Seashore became the first park of its kind.

The park includes the southern part of Bodie Island, and most of Hatteras and Ocracoke Islands, excluding the villages of Rodanthe, Waves, Salvo, Avon, Buxton, Frisco, Hatteras and Ocracoke. It offers visitors nearly 70 miles of primitive beach with visitor centers and camping areas. N.C. Highway 12 traverses the park.

KILL DEVIL HILLS

Site of Man's First Powered Flight

The Wright brothers, Wilber and Orville, bicycle shop owners and tinkerers from Dayton, Ohio, first became interested in the idea of manned flight near the end of the 19th century. In 1900, when Wilber was 33, Orville 29, they built a glider and began looking for a place with appropriate winds to test it.

They chose the windswept sand dunes of North Carolina's Outer Banks, and in the fall of that year, they set up camp near Kill Devil Hills and began their experiments. They returned each fall for the next two years with new gliders and broke all records for glider experiments at that time: largest flown, longest in the air, smallest angle of descent, flight in highest wind. They also built the first wind tunnel to use in their experiments.

Those experiments convinced them that a motor-powered, manned craft could fly, and in 1903 they built such a craft and returned to Kill Devil Hills with it that fall. They suffered many problems and frustrations, causing them to stay longer than usual. But on December 14, with Wilber at the controls, their spindly craft almost cleared the wooden launching ramp before it stalled.

They were certain it would fly, however, and after a day of repairs to the machine and another day of waiting for the right winds, they made another attempt. At 10:35 a.m., December 17, their plane carried Orville aloft for 12 seconds, a distance of 100 feet, man's first flight in a powered craft. They took turns flying it three more times that morning. The last flight carried Wilber 852 feet in 57 seconds. Soon after the

Site of man's first powered flight
Wright Brothers Memorial

flights, a gust of wind caught the unanchored plane and flipped it end over end, wrecking it.

The Wright Brothers Memorial, an imposing granite structure on a dune overlooking the site of the first flight, is on U.S. Highway 158 bypass at milepost 7. The visitors' center and museum contains a full-scale model of the Wrights' first plane. Their camp and the wooden runway have been reconstructed at the original site. The memorial is open daily, 8–6:30, in summer; 8:30–4:30 the rest of the year.

Man Will Never Fly
Memorial Society Dinner

The Man Will Never Fly Memorial Society was organized in 1959 to counter the annual observance of Wilber and Orville Wright's first flight of a powered craft on the dunes of Kill Devil Hills on December 17, 1903.

The society believes that the first flight was faked and as a result a massive fraud is being perpetuated.

"The society contends that deep down inside we all know that no machine made of tons of metal is going to 'fly,'" the society says.

But because of the Wright brothers, "people have been soaring into—and plummeting from—the skies ever since because they believe it can be done. We contend that is faith—faith misplaced and resulting from a deliberate fraud.

"How many unexplained air crashes are there and in how many of these did the pilot say to himself, 'Son of a gun—the Man Will Never Fly Memorial Society is right. This thing can't possibly fly.'? Crash. More headlines."

The society's slogan is "Birds fly—men drink." Its pledge is: "Given a choice we will never fly: given no choice we will never fly sober." The society numbers 5,000 members. Membership is $2 for a lifetime. Each year on December 16, the society holds a dinner to present awards for dubious achievements in aviation. For more information, write the society at P.O. Box 1903, Kill Devil Hills, N.C. 27948.

MANTEO

America's Oldest Symphonic Outdoor Drama

The Lost Colony, the story of the mysterious disappearance of the first English settlement in the New World, became America's first symphonic outdoor drama when it opened July 4, 1937. President Franklin D. Roosevelt came to see the show the following month.

The drama, which at the end of the 1983 season had attendance of nearly 2.5 million since its opening, was written by North Carolina playwright Paul Green, who won a Pulitzer Prize in 1927 for his first play, *In Abraham's Bosom*. Green, who wrote several Broadway hits and movies, became known as the father of outdoor drama and wrote several others after *The Lost Colony*.

The drama has been presented every year since 1937, except for two years during World War II when the coast was blacked out, at the Waterside Theater at Ft. Raleigh National Historic Site on Roanoke

An important moment in Paul Green's THE LOST COLONY—
the first outdoor drama of its kind—is this scene set in Plymouth, England.
Here, Sir Walter Raleigh bids farewell to the brave band of settlers
who are about to sail for their new home in what would eventually
become North Carolina. The epic drama has been staged
by veteran Broadway/Hollywood director Joe Layton.
It is presented on the spot where the colony settled and vanished,
Roanoke Island on the Outer Banks.
Photo: J. Foster Scott

Island, where the first English settlement was attempted. The site is off U.S. Highway 64. The play is presented nightly except Sunday at 8:30 p.m. from June 15 through September 1.

Andy Griffith, who has a home in Manteo, played Sir Walter Raleigh in the drama before going on to stardom and still attends at least one performance every year. Joe Layton, multiple-award winning director and choreographer, with many Broadway and movie successes to his credit, has directed and choreographed *The Lost Colony* since 1964.

World's Largest Wooden Sculpture

R. K. Harniman was among the first to use a chain saw as a sculpting tool. In 1974, Harniman, who called himself "The Tree Carver," was hired by a Raleigh shopping mall to create a tree sculpture as a mall attraction. Harniman decided to carve Sir Walter Raleigh. This is how the decision was made:

"Just drinking beer. Somebody said Raleigh. Sir Walter Raleigh. That was it. I never plan anything in my life."

Harniman flew over an eastern N.C. forest in a lumber company helicopter to select the right tree for the project. He spotted Sir Walter hunkering upside down in the upper reaches of a 120-foot-tall cypress. The tree, 507 years old by ring count, was cut and a huge chunk of it was hauled to the Raleigh mall where Harniman spent ten months sawing and chiseling a figure from it.

He said that the figure was Sir Walter, but spectators often noted that it looked more like R. K. Harniman.

The statue, which Harniman claimed to be the world's largest wooden sculpture, stands 24 feet tall and weighs 15,000 pounds. It was donated to the town of Manteo, where Sir Walter established his first colony, and erected on the town's waterfront in Bicentennial Park. World's largest wooden sculpture or not, some residents have called it an eyesore.

America's Oldest Grapevine

America's original wine is believed to have been made from the sweet golden scuppernong grapes of an ancient vine. Some contend that this Mother Vine was planted by the first English settlers in America, the famed Lost Colony. Others say the vine, which still bears fruit, is at least 300 years old. Records show that the vine was old in the 1750s. A

World's largest wooden sculpture: Sir Walter Raleigh

vineyard and small winery were developed around the vine earlier in this century, but the area is now an exclusive housing development.

The gnarled and twisted vine is on private property just east of Manteo on Mother Vineyard Road off U.S. Highway 64. The vine is on the left about 300 feet past where the road takes a sharp turn at the bay.

America's Oldest Working Tugboat

If there is an older working tugboat in America than the *Lookout*, Harry Schiffman hasn't been able to find it. Harry, who operates the Salty Dog Marina on a creek behind Manteo Middle School, found the tug in the swampy headwaters of the Alligator River in 1981. The boat, which had been used to push log barges, had been out of service a couple of years. The company that owned it was bankrupt.

The *Lookout*, Harry discovered, had been built of cold steel in Camden, N.J., in 1862, equipped with a steam engine and used to haul ammunition to Yankee soldiers during the Civil War.

Harry rebuilt the 61-foot boat, which long ago had its steam engine replaced with a diesel engine, and is now using it to haul road building materials from the mainland to the Outer Banks. When it's not tugging or pushing, the old boat can be seen at Salty Dog Marina.

The Lookout, oldest tug in America
Photo: J. Foster Scott

Andy Griffith's Tree Farm

Andy Griffith, who was born in Mt. Airy, was a high school English teacher in Goldsboro. He appeared in *The Lost Colony* outdoor drama in summer and frequently did comedy routines for civic groups, when he cut a comedy record called "What It Was Was Football," recorded at an insurance company dinner in Greensboro.

The record sold more than a million copies, got Andy appearances in major night clubs and led to his first big movie role in *No Time for Sergeants*.

Although he has appeared in numerous movies and TV shows, Andy's biggest success came in the long-running "Andy Griffith Show," a TV classic, in which he played Sheriff Andy Taylor of fictional Mayberry, North Carolina. The show, still tops in re-runs, has spawned many fan clubs and even a book.

Soon after Andy achieved financial success, he bought a house and 57 acres on Roanoke Sound. There he started a tree farm and now makes his summer home. The modest house is visible from the water but not from a public road. Andy's trees, however, are visible alongside U.S. Highway 64, about three-fourths of a mile south of the Airport Road, north of Manteo. Visitors are not received.

NAGS HEAD

Ghost Ship

Residents of the Outer Banks awoke on the morning of January 31, 1921, to see a beautiful five-masted sailing vessel aground on a sandbar at treacherous Diamond Shoals, where many ships had met their end.

Strangely, no distress signals were flying from the ship, but two lifesaving crews struck out for the ship anyway to remove the crew. Seas proved too heavy for them to reach the ship, and they had to turn back. They did get close enough to see the ship's name, Carroll A. Deering, but they were surprised that no crew members were to be seen on deck.

Lifesavers finally reached the ship next morning to find no crew at all, only a cat. Food had been cooked, the table prepared for the crew's meal, but nobody had eaten. Nothing seemed amiss, except for a missing lifeboat and some disorder among the captain's maps.

The crew was never found and no bodies ever washed ashore. Several weeks after the ship ran aground, it was dynamited as a hazard to navigation, but residents of the Outer Banks still talk about the mystery of the ghost ship.

In 1982, Melvin Kooker, owner of a commercial haunted house in Virginia Beach, built a landlocked model of the Carroll A. Deering at milepost 16 on the U.S. Highway 158 bypass at Nags Head and opened it as "The Ghost Ship."

The five-masted, triple-decked model, 110 feet long, provides the setting for the retelling of the story of the Deering with live actors to visitors who are guided through the ship. It is open Memorial Day to Labor Day for a fee.

Lynanne Wescott's Windmill

At one time more than 200 windmills whirled on the Outer Banks, grinding grain for settlers, but all of them disappeared.

Lynanne Wescott saw a picture of one of those while browsing through a history book and was so taken with its beauty that she embarked on a year's research of Outer Banks windmills. At the end of that year, she decided to build one of her own.

She chose the old mill that once stood at Buxton as her model, and four years later she finished her replica of it. It was 35 feet tall with a grinding house 9 feet by 12. Its four blades, 15 feet long and 6 feet wide, were covered with linen sailcloth.

Lynanne got the windmill operating in November, 1981, and it became the only commercial grain-grinding windmill in America. But in July, 1982, Lynanne was transferred to Philadelphia by the National Parks Service and that fall she had to sell her property on the Outer Banks, including—reluctantly—her windmill.

The new owners closed the windmill and late in 1983 its fate was uncertain, although Lynanne was sure it wouldn't be dismantled. It stands by the sound, just off the U.S. Highway 158 bypass.

America's Highest Sand Dune

Jockey's Ridge, a towering sand dune just off the U.S. Highway 158 bypass, is a freak of nature created by man's meddling with the environment. Early settlers on the Outer Banks, as North Carolina's fragile barrier islands are called, cut trees and allowed stock to overgraze. Wind erosion began shifting exposed sands and the huge dune built

Lynanne Wescott's windmill

gradually until it was more than 100 feet tall. At times the dune, which is continually moving westward, is as tall as 125 feet.

The dune provides a magnificent view of island, sound and sea and has been a tourist attraction since the 19th century. Legend once held that the woman who accompanied a man to its summit would soon become his wife.

In the early '70s, local residents became alarmed by development near the dune, and the property was purchased and made into a state park in 1975.

Hang gliders regularly provide a colorful spectacle at the dune, and each year in May, the Hang Gliding Spectacular, a three-day competition, is held. Hang gliding enthusiasts occasionally have the opportunity to meet the man who made their sport possible. Francis Rogallo, who invented the hang glider while doing research on space capsule re-entry for NASA, lives nearby and frequently visits the dune. For more information on the Hang Gliding Spectacular, write John Harris, P.O. Box 340, Nags Head, N.C. 27959, or call (919) 441-6094.

Hang gliding off America's highest sand dune
Photo: Kitty Hawk Kites

RODANTHE

Old Christmas

Outer Bankers have always been independent and Old Christmas is evidence of that.

When King George ordered England and its colonies to switch from the Julian to the Gregorian calendar in 1752, thus losing 11 days, Outer Bankers rebelled and continued to celebrate Christmas on the old day, which then fell on January 5.

The tradition has continued. Now Old Christmas is celebrated on the Saturday closest to January 5 (so long as it doesn't fall on New Year's weekend) with a shooting match, oyster roast, chicken stew and square dance at the Rodanthe Community Center.

Highlight of the occasion is the traditional appearance of Ol' Buck, a mythical maverick steer that could never be found during open-range roundups. "Be good," generations of Outer Banks children have been told, "or Ol' Buck will get you." Buck shows up once a year just as a reminder.

In years past, Old Christmas celebrations were a bit rowdy. "There used to be more fighting," one resident remembers. "They would fight until the last man would fall."

SALVO

The Second-Smallest Post Office
In America

The Salvo Post Office on N.C. Highway 12 attracts a lot of attention. A frame building 8 feet by 12, it was built shortly after the turn of the century and has been in continuous service since. It contains boxes for 94 patrons and sitting room for postmaster Edward Hooper, a Salvo native born in 1922.

Many travelers think it must be the smallest post office in America and stop to find out. It isn't.

The post office in Ochopee, Florida, in the Everglades is only 7 feet by 8, leaving Salvo second in smallness. That doesn't keep people from taking snapshots of it, though. "I have my picture made so much I feel like a model," says Hooper.

Postmaster Edward Hooper and America's second-smallest post office

DUPLIN

KENANSVILLE

The House Where Henry Flagler Married

Liberty Hall, a plantation house, was built in 1830 by Thomas Kenan II, a member of one of North Carolina's most prominent early families. By the turn of the century, the house had passed to Mary Lily Kenan, a friend of Henry Flagler, one-time partner of John D. Rockefeller, railroad owner and developer of South Florida.

In 1901, Flagler, then 71 and twice married, asked Mary Lily, then 34, to marry him, and Liberty Hall became the site of North Carolina's most famous wedding.

Legend has it that Flagler built a railroad spur to Kenansville in order to whisk away his bride in his private railroad car. He built Mary Lily a marble palace in Palm Beach, and she went there to live, leaving Liberty Hall to fall into disrepair.

The house has since been restored and may be toured for a small fee. Mary Lily's wedding dress is on display. The house is on N.C. Highway 24 in Kenansville and is open Tuesday–Saturday, 10–4, Sunday, 2–4. For more information call (919) 296-0522.

ROSE HILL

Grape Stomp

Before the Civil War, North Carolina was the nation's leading wine making state. The 1840 census showed more than 6,000 acres of vineyards in the state, with 33 wineries producing more than a million gallons of wine, primarily from native muscadine grapes.

The Civil War ended wine production in the state, and although it revived later, Prohibition knocked it for another loop in the '20s. But interest in wine production began to revive again in the 60's, and now the state boasts three wineries—one at Biltmore House in Asheville bottling estate wines, a tiny one at Germantown near Winston-Salem, and by far the biggest, the Duplin Wine Cellars in Rose Hill.

David Fussell, a former high school principal and part-time grape grower, started Duplin Wine Cellars as a farmers co-op in 1972, and its first wines went to market in 1976. The winery makes wines ranging from sweet to dry using native grapes, and even makes a North Carolina champagne from a 200-year-old recipe.

Each year at harvest in late September (the weekends may vary) the winery holds an open house with tastings and champagne-making demonstration and a grape-stomping contest.

Contestants in the grape stomp climb into big wooden vats holding measured amounts of grapes and stomp for one minute. The contestant producing the most juice is the winner. Don't worry about the juice from the contest ending up in your wine.

"It's thrown away," says a company spokesman. "We don't make anybody drink it."

For more information call the winery at (919) 289-3094.

World's Largest Frying Pan

Dennis Ramsey, owner of a feed company in Rose Hill, was visiting poultry producers in Maryland when he saw what was claimed to be the world's largest frying pan. It was about 10 feet in diameter, and local poultry producers used it for big chicken frys.

Ramsey decided that Rose Hill, another poultry center, should have a bigger pan for the annual N.C. Poultry Producers Jubilee, which had just begun in the town. He instructed one of his employees to build it.

Clarence Brown remembers working on the pan with a couple of other employees off and on for about six months. They built it of quarter-inch steel in eight pie-shaped wedges so that it would be portable. They made it 15 feet in diameter, 6 inches deep and added a 7-foot handle.

Forty gas burners are required to fire the pan, which is capable of frying more than 250 chickens at once.

The pan is now permanently mounted under a shelter in Little League Park on Sycamore Street (U.S. Highway 117). It is used for frying chicken during Rose Hill's Fall Jamboree, held around the first weekend in October, which replaced the Poultry Jubilee in 1983.

GATES

GATESVILLE

Oldest Living Things?

A stand of two dozen virgin cypress trees remains in Lassiter Swamp five miles up Bennetts Creek from Merchants Millpond State Park, about six miles east of Gatesville, off U.S. Highway 158. Nobody knows for sure, but the trees are believed to be well beyond 1,000 years old, and some may have been standing in the time of Christ, ranking them among the oldest living things on earth. The trees may be seen by canoe, which can be rented at the park.

HALIFAX

HOLLISTER

Haliwa-Saponi Pow Wow

The Haliwa Indians, a group of about 2,500 people who took their names from the counties where they live, Halifax and Warren, trace their ancestry to the Saponi Indians who once lived in eastern North Carolina. But until 1965, when the state finally recognized them as one of five different Indian tribes in the state, they had trouble convincing people of their heritage.

Since that time, they have held a celebration every year on the third weekend in April to celebrate their recognition. A campfire is held on Friday night and on Saturday comes the crowning of the Haliwa-Saponi princess, native dances and demonstrations of beadwork and basketry.

A highly acclaimed treat at the event is the traditional fry bread, served with honey.

For more information, call Kathy Wilson at (919) 586-4017.

HARNETT

ANGIER

Tink Coats' Bell Tower and Museum

Robert Floyd Coats, a long-time high school principal in Harnett County, was called Tink because he loved to tinker with all sorts of things. Gadgets fascinated him and so did old tools and other instruments. But nothing fascinated him more than bells. During his lifetime, he collected dozens of bells, from little tinklers to big bongers four feet across.

A bell isn't much good if it can't be rung, and Tink wanted to ring his. So in 1968, at age 81, Tink decided to build himself a bell tower in his front yard. It took him three years and when he finished he had a magnificent tower, built of steel, 55 feet tall with a base 15 feet by 20, anchored in concrete 12 feet deep. From the tower hung 32 bells, ranging from 1 foot in width to nearly 5 feet. From each hung a rope, and Tink could ring his bells to his heart's content.

In 1972, Tink completed a building next to his house for his antiques museum, and it became a community gathering spot. Each year until his death in 1976 at age 85, Tink held community bell ringings on Easter, Independence Day and New Year's Eve.

Tink's great-nephew, Tim Penny, who now lives in his house,

continues the tradition, and he and his wife, Vicki, keep Tink's museum open to visitors on weekends and special occasions. Tim, an avid fan of the University of North Carolina football team, has begun his own tradition of ringing the bells after every Carolina touchdown.

The bell tower is on State Road 1309, .8 of a mile off N.C. Highway 210, six miles southeast of Angier. To see the museum by special appointment call Tim at (919) 894-4532.

ERWIN

World's Largest and Smallest Pairs of Blue Jeans

The town of Erwin grew around a cotton mill that produced denim for the overalls of eastern North Carolina farmers. That plant, now part of Burlington Industries, has become the world's largest producer of denim and the primary employer in Erwin. To acknowledge that, Erwin holds a Denim Days celebration each year on the second weekend in October.

If you don't wear jeans or some other form of denim on Denim Days, you can be locked up in a mock jail.

To help celebrate, there are beauty pageants, a rodeo, a fishing contest, a water ski show, a craft show, sky-diving exhibitions, and contests to pick the best designers and makers of denim outfits.

In front of the denim plant on Burlington Avenue, the world's largest roll of denim, more than 6 feet tall and 5 feet wide, is displayed along with the world's largest and smallest pairs of jeans. The largest jeans have a 72-inch waist and are more than 10 feet long. The smallest have only a 2-inch waist, appropriate for a small doll.

For more information call Clarence Lee at (919) 897-8111.

HYDE

OCRACOKE

Wild Banker Ponies

At one time more than 1,000 small wild horses roamed Ocracoke Island and Cape Hatteras. How they came to be there is a mystery. Some believe the horses were descended from stock brought by the first colonists. Others think they came from Spanish shipwrecks, a more likely case, since scientific tests have proved that the russet-colored horses came from Spanish mustangs. Once, the horses were regularly rounded up and sold. Now fewer than two dozen remain and they are kept penned by the National Park Service on the west side of N.C. Highway 12 between the Hatteras Ferry and Ocracoke village.

The Whelk Lady's Exotic Shells
And Rare Birds

Alta Van Landingham, whose grandfather was keeper of the Ocracoke lighthouse, moved from California to be near her ailing father after he retired to the island where he'd grown up. Soon after settling on the island, Alta returned to a childhood pleasure: roaming the beach collecting shells. After collecting all of the 300 species to be found on Ocracoke, she expanded her horizons. She and husband, Van, a retired Marine, began traveling up and down the East Coast searching for new shells.

To help pay for her hobby, Alta opened a small shell shop next to her house on N.C. Highway 12 on the eastern edge of Ocracoke village. Alta's shell collection now includes nearly 7,000 species from around the world. In her living room, Alta keeps numerous living shell creatures in 35 aquariums ranging from 10 to 200 gallons in size. She came to be called the Whelk Lady after she did a serious, long-term study of whelks, large sea snails, that she raised in her aquariums. Her shell collection and aquariums may be seen by visitors, and her husband's collection of nearly 100 exotic birds, which he keeps in the house and shell shop, adds noise and color to the experience.

JOHNSTON

BENSON

America's Largest and Oldest Gospel Singing

Back in 1921, five of Benson's most prominent business and civic leaders got to talking about how much they loved gospel music and decided they'd just have a big singing at a tobacco warehouse.

They had such a good time that they decided to make it an annual event. It grew so popular that the family that founded Benson deeded the town a complete downtown block to be called the Singing Grove and provide a place for the annual event, which came to be called the North Carolina State Singing Convention.

The free event, held every year since 1921, is on the weekend of the fourth Sunday in June. It is now a two-day event, beginning at 2 p.m. Saturday and continuing through Sunday afternoon.

More than 100 groups of singers appear every year to compete for trophies and more than 50,000 people turn out to hear them.

"Some of the groups kind of modernize it a little bit," says P. B. Wood, president of the association that stages the singing, "but mostly it's just good ol' Southern gospel."

Mule Day

In 1950, when Benson first held Mule Day, mule teams could still be seen working in the vast flat farmlands surrounding the town. Folks in town wanted to do something to honor these faithful workers, so they staged Mule Day and farmers from several counties came with their mules. Hundreds of mules paraded through the streets and competed in contests.

But as the years passed, mules disappeared from the fields and fewer showed up for Mule Day. Then in the mid-1970s came a turn-around. Mules were rediscovered. People started raising them for fun, to pull wagon trains and take to special events. Now more than 1,000 mules show up in Benson on the last Saturday in September to parade and compete in beauty contests, pulling events and races. Hundreds of horses show up, too.

In addition to the mule events, there are a rodeo and a street dance. Dancers are advised to watch their step.

SMITHFIELD

Ava Gardner Museum

When Tom Banks was 10, growing up in Wilson, playing on the campus of Atlantic Christian College, he used to banter with a pretty student who waited each day for a ride near the spot where he played. He couldn't have imagined then that one day that bantering would result in one of North Carolina's more unusual museums.

Tom didn't learn the pretty girl's name until some time after she had disappeared from the campus. Then he saw her picture in the news-paper one day with the startling revelation that she was marrying movie star Mickey Rooney. The pretty student Tom had called his girlfriend was about to become a big movie star herself. Her name was Ava Gardner.

Later, Tom wrote to Ava in Hollywood, reminding her of those days at Atlantic Christian. She answered and said she remembered him. They exchanged several letters and when Tom went away to college, Ava agreed to be sweetheart of his fraternity.

After college, Tom went to Hollywood himself and worked as a publicist on one of Ava's pictures, *My Forbidden Past*. He moved on to become a publicist for Columbia Pictures in New York before returning to school to get his doctorate in psychology and settling into a practice in Ft. Lauderdale, Florida.

But Tom still kept up with Ava and her career. He began collecting material about her, and he compiled scrapbooks for each year of her career, gathered more than 10,000 still photographs from her movie sets, and collected posters and audio cassettes from every movie and video cassettes from most of them.

When Tom visited Ava in London in the late '70s, he told her that he wanted to give his collection to an institution in her honor. She suggested it should be in North Carolina, her home state. Tom was thinking of giving it to a college until he visited Johnston County to see Ava's birthplace.

The big house where Ava was born in the Brogden community six miles east of Smithfield was still standing but in disrepair. The teacherage where she lived from ages 2 to 13 while her mother taught school was being used as a community social hall. In 1981, Tom bought the teacherage, renovated it, moved his collection into it and opened the Ava Gardner Museum in 1982.

Each summer an Ava Festival is held with her movies shown continuously at no charge. The rest of the year the museum may be seen by appointment. Call Doris Cannon at (919) 934-2176.

NASH

BAILEY

Country Doctor Museum

In rural North Carolina, the country doctor was a greatly revered and highly depended upon person. Almost always male, he often covered a large territory, did much of his work in his patients' homes and treated every ailment known or imagined.

Doctors in rural areas are like other doctors now, seeing patients only in their offices or hospitals, but the memory of the old-time doctors lives on at the Country Doctor Museum on Vance Street in Bailey.

The museum was created in 1968, ironically by four female doctors, Josephine Newell, Gloria Graham, Rose Pulley and Josephine

Melchior, all from medical families. All of them had old medical equipment that had been passed down to them, and they thought it ought to be preserved and displayed.

Two old doctor's offices were moved to the site and joined to create the three-room museum. One room is a replica of an old-time doctor's office. Another is a pharmacy, and the third contains old equipment ranging from early stethoscopes and microscopes to primitive dental equipment and bleeding instruments. Behind the museum is an herb garden that is a replica of the Medicinal Garden in Padua, Italy. The free museum is open Wednesday and Sunday, 2–5. It may be seen other times by appointment. Call Joyce Cooper at (919) 478-5716.

NEW HANOVER

KURE BEACH

Oldest Fishing Pier on the East Coast

L. C. Kure built the first fishing pier into the Atlantic Ocean in 1923, using timbers cut nearby. The pier was 16 feet wide and 120 feet long, and it fell in a storm the first year.

The following year, Kure rebuilt his pier with concrete posts reinforced with railroad iron, doubling the length and width. It has since been damaged by hurricanes 11 times and rebuilt every time.

In 1952, Bill Robertson, then Kure's son-in-law, bought the Pier and with relentless promotion made it into a big attraction, the most popular fishing pier on the coast. Three phenomenal months of fishing in the fall of 1957 didn't hurt any. People hauled fish off the pier in wheelbarrows. In a single day more than 80,000 fish were caught from the pier.

Bill has hundreds of stories about the pier and loves telling them. Many he put into a book, the title of which he took from a sign that hangs over the pier entrance: "Man! You Should Have Been Here Last Week."

SEABREEZE

World's Oldest Elephant

Although they are generally believed to be long-lived creatures, elephants in the wild live less than 50 years. In captivity, they sometimes live longer. Matteau, a female Asian elephant, was 55 when George Tregembo traded four rheas, South American ostrichlike birds, for her in 1966. She turned 72 in December, 1983, and the Elephant Interest Group says that makes her the oldest elephant in America and one of the oldest that ever lived. The greatest confirmed age for an elephant is 70 years, but an elephant that died in a California amusement park was believed to be 78.

Matteau, who weighs nearly five tons, is a familiar sight alongside U.S. Highway 421 south of Wilmington, where during daylight hours in spring, summer and fall, she serves as an attention grabber for George Tregembo's Tote-Em-In Zoo and house of wonders.

George grew up in Maine with dreams of collecting curiosities and exotic animals. He started collecting relics and oddities when he fought in the South Pacific during World War II. When he returned home, he opened a small roadside attraction, but because of bad weather and few tourists, he moved to North Carolina in 1953.

At that time, his zoo had 21 species. It now has 130. His collections of oddities fill several buildings and include relics of primitive people from the South Pacific, Africa, South America and Alaska, war materiel, Presidential chairs, ancient art objects and natural wonders such as fossilized dinosaur footprints and the world's largest moth.

A single fee is charged for entrance to the zoo and his collections. Matteau, a gentle creature, can be seen for free. Her handler, James Dinkins, who is the same age as Matteau, sells vegetables for visitors to feed her. Matteau likes almost all fruits and vegetables but refuses peanuts.

"She'll just take 'em and throw 'em down," says George. "She says, 'I'm not working for peanuts.'"

George Tregembo and Matteau, world's oldest elephant
Photo: Greensboro News-Record

Thalian Hall, oldest little theater in America

WILMINGTON

Oldest Little Theater in America

The Thalian Society, founded in 1788, is the oldest amateur theater group in America. It is the resident company of Thalian Hall, one of America's oldest opera houses. The hall, which faces Princess Street, is a wing of the white-columned City Hall on Third Street.

The theater, with its double balconies and elaborate gilded ornamentation, has seen performances by Lillian Russell, Buffalo Bill Cody, John Philip Sousa, Oscar Wilde, Marian Anderson and the Ziegfeld Follies. The ghost of one performer who played there, James O'Neill, famous actor of the last century and father of playwright Eugene O'Neill, is believed to haunt the theater.

"I've never seen him and I don't think anybody has," says the theater's assistant director, Phillip Cumber, "but we've heard him bumping and thumping around."

Strange things are always happening at the theater and are inevitably blamed on James.

Seances have been held to try to rouse James and other ghosts, but none has succeeded. During a rehearsal in 1966, though, cast members saw three figures clad in Victorian clothing watching from the upper balcony. When company members got to the balcony to investigate, the figures were gone but three seats were turned down as if somebody had been sitting in them.

Tours of the theater are available Tuesday–Saturday, 10–5, for a small fee. For information about productions call (919) 763-3398, or write the Thalian Society, 2022 Washington Street, Wilmington, N.C. 28401.

The Children's Battleship

The Battleship U.S.S. *North Carolina* was headed for the scrap heap when school children all across the state joined in a campaign to save it in the early '60s. The money they raised helped bring the ship to the state as a memorial to veterans.

Now permanently docked on the Cape Fear River across from downtown Wilmington, the *North Carolina*, which fought in the major Pacific battles of World War II, may be toured for a small fee. From June through Labor Day, a sound and light show telling the ship's history is

Children's battleship, U.S.S. North Carolina

presented nightly at 9 for an extra fee. Signs direct the way to the ship from U.S. Highways 421 and 17.

Girl Buried in Keg of Rum

In 1857, Silas Martin, a ship's captain, set out from Wilmington on an around-the-world voyage. With him went his 34-year-old son John and 24-year-old daughter Nancy, whose pet family name was Nance. At sea, Nancy grew sick and died. Her grieving father had her body folded into a barrel of rum so that it would be preserved until he could bury her at home.

Before Captain Martin could get back, his son was washed overboard during a storm and lost, his body never recovered despite a long search. When Martin finally did make it back to Wilmington, he buried his daughter still in the cask of rum. He was buried beside her four years later.

Nance's grave in Oakdale Cemetery is marked with a stone made to resemble a cross made of logs, next to the larger family marker. The cemetery, which contains many other interesting graves dating back to 1855, is at 520 North 15th Street. The most interesting graves have special markers, and a free itinerary of them may be picked up at the cemetery office at the entrance.

Grave of Nancy Martin, girl buried in keg of rum
Photo: Greensboro News-Record

Southeast's Largest Collection of Old Work Boats

This collection of a half-dozen boats was assembled as the focal point of a riverfront development of tourist shops and restaurants called Chandler's Wharf. The collection includes the double-masted Nova Scotia cargo and fishing schooner *Harry D. Adams*, the quarantine boat *Eugene Wasdin*, the shrimp boat *Miss Santa*, the log boat *Edward M* (built from five hollowed-out logs), the excursion boat *J. N. Maffit*, and the tugboat *John Taxis*, built in 1869 and proclaimed by the owners to be the oldest tug in America (it isn't; an older tug, the *Lookout*, built in 1862, can be seen in Manteo, still working). A fee is charged to view the boats. A riverfront tour in the *J. N. Maffit* is available at additional charge.

America's Largest Living Christmas Tree

Every year since 1929, city workers have spent days stringing lights and Spanish moss on a 300-year-old water oak to serve as the community Christmas tree. The 80-foot-tall tree has a limb spread of 110 feet, and nearly 5,000 colored lights are required to decorate it. For more than half a century, Wilmington has proclaimed it America's largest living Christmas tree. The tree, on U.S. Highway 117, two blocks north of Fourth Street, is lighted nightly from the second week in December until New Year's Day.

ONSLOW

JACKSONVILLE

World's Oldest Putt Putt

The Putt Putt miniature golf course on LeJeune Boulevard was the second built and is the oldest in existence. Putt Putt creator Don Clayton built the course in the fall of 1954. A metal sign he nailed onto a pine tree offering a free pass for a hole-in-one on hole 18 is still there, now imbedded into the tree that grew around it. For more on Putt Putt, see Fayetteville in Cumberland County.

PAMLICO

ORIENTAL

Croaker Festival

Croakers are small saltwater fish that make a strange croaking noise when removed from the water. Favored for the taste and texture of their flesh, they are common in North Carolina coastal waters.

Unfortunately, they aren't common at all when Oriental, a quaint town known more for sailing than fishing, holds its Croaker Festival. But the ladies of Oriental's Junior Woman's Club didn't realize that when they started their festival on July 4th weekend in 1978 and made a croaker fishing contest one of the events.

"We didn't know croakers are not running that time of the year," says Linda Carrow, one of the organizers. "All you can catch are these little tiny ones."

So the fishing contest was dropped and that left almost no role in the festivities for croakers at all. Even the Methodist church fish fry features trout.

But the Junior Woman's Club forges gamely on with its croaker-less salute to croakers nonetheless, staging beauty contests, raft and canoe races, an arts and crafts show, a street dance and other entertainments. Sailing races are also held in conjunction with the event. For more information, call Linda Carrow at (919) 249-1808.

PASQUOTANK

ELIZABETH CITY

Soybean Festival

It's not easy to build a festival around soybeans. After all, they're used primarily for making cooking oil, feeding livestock and making vegetable meal to be added to other food products. You can't put on a soybean supper and draw much of a crowd.

Some years back, somebody got the idea that roasted soybeans might sell as well as roasted peanuts. They didn't. And you can find out why by sampling some at the Soybean Festival.

Still, it seemed like a good idea for Elizabeth City to honor soybeans, because the first commercial plantings of the oriental crop in the United States were made near the town in the last century, and the first soybean processing plant in the country was built here in 1912. Soybeans have since become one of the state's and nation's biggest crops and a primary export commodity.

"It's quite a lot to celebrate and commemorate," says Don Baker, a county farm agent who helped organize the event.

The festival is held on the first Saturday in December at the Albemarle 4-H Livestock Arena on U.S. Highway 17, one mile south of Elizabeth City. Farm equipment is displayed and country music is performed. For more information, call Don Baker at (919) 338-3954.

PENDER

HAMSTEAD

Mac Millis's Outer Space Venus-Flytrap Nursery

The Venus-flytrap, the most dramatic of all the earth's insect-eating plants, grows naturally in only one place, an area within about a 75-mile radius of Hamstead. McKinley Millis, usually called Mac, remembers playing with them as a child growing up on Harrison Creek, sticking sticks into them, trying to make their spine-like teeth shut, the way the plant traps insects to devour.

"We called 'em eye catchers," Mac remembers. "Looked like a person's eye."

Mac was born in 1911, and in the days of his boyhood livestock was allowed to range freely and crops were fenced. Woods were burned regularly to clear undergrowth and create forage for the stock. Burning the woods created a prime environment for the Venus-flytrap, which grew prolifically in the cleared, damp areas.

The plant, now protected by law, is endangered due to poaching, development, modern tree farming techniques and other factors, and seeing one in the wild is a rare treat. But plenty are to be seen at Mac Millis's small nursery on U.S. Highway 17 at the intersection of N.C. Highway 210 (the nursery is named for Mac's daughter, Marie).

Mac began experimenting with growing flytraps from seeds nearly 30 years ago and became one of the first commercial growers of the plant. How he grows them, he won't tell.

"I got a lot of secrets I don't give out," he says.

Mac, incidentally, believes that the plant got its name because the seed actually came from Venus.

Southeastern North Carolina is dotted with mysterious, shallow, round craters, most of them water-filled, called the Carolina Bays. Some scientists believe the craters were caused by a meteor shower long ago, and Mac believes that.

"My great-great-granddaddy remembered when they fell," he says.

He also believes that the seeds of the flytrap, a plant with a space-monsterish look about it, arrived on those meteors by way of Venus.

If there are flytraps on Venus, there must be flies there, too, right?

"I guess so," says Mac. "No telling what's there. Nobody never been there to find out, have they?"

Spot Festival

The spots celebrated in Hamstead every year aren't the kind you see in front of your eyes when you're dizzy, or the kind you get on your clothes when you drip ketchup or gravy. These are the spots that swim in the ocean, the ones you can eat, and eating is the major event of the Spot Festival.

The spot is the most bountiful fish in North Carolina's coastal waters. Spots are small, silver-colored, with a distinctive black spot near the gills. They are a favorite of sports fishermen who sometimes catch them by the bucketsfull, especially in spring and fall.

Spots weren't caught commercially until the '30s, but by the '50s they had become the biggest selling fish in the South.

Three seafood packing plants grew in Hamstead, processing tons of spots every year. In 1964, to draw attention to the community's claim of being "the seafood capital of the Carolinas," and celebrate the beginning of the fall run of spots, the Spot Festival was begun to raise money for community projects.

Held on the first weekend in October, the festival is a three-day event with beauty pageants, a golf tournament, pig picking, an arts and crafts show, an auction and entertainment by popular groups. But the big event is the fish fry at the community building, which begins at 11 a.m. on Saturday and continues until 6 p.m. More than 3,500 pounds of spots are cooked. For more information call Ruth Jones at (919) 686-9641.

SCOTT'S HILL

Haunted Plantation

From 1795 until 1975, Poplar Grove Plantation was in the Foy family. In the early 1800s, Poplar Grove became one of North Carolina's first and biggest peanut-producing plantations. The original house burned and was rebuilt in 1850 by Joseph M. Foy, a wealthy and influential man in the state. His son, Joseph T. Foy, took over the plantation at age 15 upon his father's death.

In 1975, the plantation was bought by a non-profit foundation which restored it as a national historic site and opened it to tours. But one member of the Foy family refuses to move.

She is Aunt Nora, wife of the young Joseph Foy. She moved into the house as a young woman following the Civil War and lived there until her death in 1923. Nora was a lively young woman who etched her name and her husband's into a window pane of the house on their wedding day. In later years, Nora became a pipe-smoking, joke-cracking character who was community postmistress. Since her death, her presence has continued to pervade Poplar Grove. She can sometimes be heard pacing in her upstairs room. Staff members tell of tricks that Aunt Nora, as she is known, sometimes plays on them. And occasionally, when all lights are out in the house, a mysterious glow can be seen in the window of Nora's room, particularly near Christmas.

Each year at Halloween, the Plantation conducts haunted house tours and other events in honor of Aunt Nora, including a dinner featuring such dishes as sliced tongue and beef hearts with blood gravy and slime pie. The Plantation is on U.S. Highway 17, north of Wilmington. For more information call Nancy Simon at (919) 686-9886.

Poplar Grove, haunted plantation

PERQUIMANS

HERTFORD

Oldest House in North Carolina

A brick house on a rise within sight of the Perquimans River, built about 1685 by Joseph Scott, an early Quaker who became a magistrate and legislator, is the oldest house in North Carolina.

The Governors Council met at the house in the 1690s, and the Colonial Assembly was convened in it in 1697.

Since then, the house has had more than 30 owners. In 1973, it was sold to the Perquimans County Restoration Association, which restored it and opened it as a historic site in 1981. Called the Newbold-White House, after later owners, it is on State Road 1336 1.5 miles off U.S. Highway 17 bypass, southeast of Hertford. Open Tuesday-Saturday, 10–4:30; Sunday, 1:30–4:30. It may be seen only by appointment from January through March.

Largest Cherrybark Oak in America

One of the largest trees in North Carolina, the cherrybark oak on Lucky Cartwright's property on State Road 1329, two miles south of the Woodville community, is the national champion of its species. The tree is 120 feet tall with a crown spread of 126 feet. Its trunk is 29 feet in circumference.

PITT

AYDEN

The Collard Festival

Ayden is probably the only town in America with collards growing on Main Street. Collards are tall, tough greens that thrive in the colder months in the South and thus are prized as a fresh vegetable when few are to be had. At one time almost every rural home in the South had a collard patch out back.

Collards have to be cooked a long time to make them tender enough to eat and it has been said that a single pot of them cooking is enough to smell up a whole county.

Despite the fact that collards grow on Main Street and Bum's Restaurant has collards on the menu every day, folks in Ayden aren't known to grow or eat more collards than anybody else. So why do they celebrate collards every year on the second weekend in September?

Blame it on a Yankee.

Lois Theuring moved to Ayden when her husband's company transferred him to nearby Greenville. She frequently wrote articles for the local weekly newspaper, the *News-Leader*. She also hated collards. In one article that she wrote about the things she liked about the South, she closed every paragraph with a disparaging remark about collards.

As it happened, some people in town were then thinking about organizing a festival to compete with nearby Grifton's highly successful Shad Festival, and a local businessman, Willis Manning, wrote a letter to the editor asking for ideas. He closed it by facetiously suggesting that Mrs. Theuring might agree to organize a collard festival.

Lois Theuring surprised everybody by doing just that. She organized the first one in 1975 and it was a great success. She moved back to Ohio the following year, and the last anybody in Ayden heard she still hated collards.

The festival she organized grows bigger every year. It includes a parade, carnival and numerous other events. The most popular event is the collard-eating contest. It usually isn't a pretty sight, since not all the contestants are able to hold their collards.

The all-time collard-eating champion is Desmond Rogers, a 340-pound pickup truck dealer from Snow Hill, who has won the contest every time he has entered. He once downed six and a quarter pounds of collards in a single sitting.

GREENVILLE

World's Largest
Flue–cured Tobacco Show and Festival

Flue-cured tobacco is tobacco that is picked one leaf at a time and barn–cured with heat, as opposed to burly tobacco, which is cut by the stalk and hung to air dry.

Pitt County produces more flue-cured tobacco than any other place on earth. It brings $60 million a year to the local economy. So it should be no surprise that the biggest show of tobacco farming equipment is held in Greenville, the Pitt County seat. And since so many farmers and their families came to the show and were looking for entertainment, the Tobacco Festival evolved from the show.

The festival, held each year in the week before Thanksgiving, features many events at many locations, including clogging, country music, pig pickings, quilt and antique shows, pipe smoking, tobacco spitting and tobacco grading contests.

But the biggest event is the naming of the Tobacco Farmer of the Year for the five-state flue-cured tobacco growing belt, and the picking of the year's most perfect bundle of tobacco, which is always on display.

For more information, call Kay Warren at (919) 757-1604.

GRIFTON

The Shad Festival

Shad are saltwater fish, members of the herring family, that, like salmon, return to spawn in the fresh water streams where they hatched. In late winter and early spring, they move by the thousands up the Neuse River and into creeks such as Pitchkettle, Grindle and Contentnea.

Two types of shad make this migration: the hickory, which averages one to two pounds, and the white (or American), which averages three pounds but grows much larger. Hickory shad are predominant.

Both varieties are prized primarily for their roe, which is traditionally fried with onions or scrambled with eggs in eastern North Carolina.

No shad can be found at the Shad Festival. The big fish fry features herring filets. The big fish stew contains rockfish. Shad, alas, are entirely too bony for most folks' taste. Festival organizers say a shad can be made edible by baking it at least six hours, thus softening the bones. Others say it takes half a day and isn't worth the effort.

Shad may or may not be good to eat, but it is a good enough excuse for Grifton, a town of 2,400 people, to hold a five-day fling the first weekend in April, as it has been doing since 1970.

The activities include a fishing contest; a fish-lying contest; canoe races; foot races; beauty pageants; a street dance; arts and crafts competition; tennis, softball and horseshoe tournaments; a barbecue, and Shad-O games, based on Bingo. For information call Janet Hasely at (919) 524-4356.

ROBESON

LUMBERTON

L. D. Todd's
Pure-blooded Peafowl Farm

To L. D. Todd there's not a bird on earth prettier than a peacock in all its strutting, tail-flaring glory. It was their beauty that prompted him to buy a couple. Next thing he knew, he had retired from his job at a dairy and was raising hundreds of peafowl yearly in a maze of chicken-wire pens next to his house on N.C. Highway 211, east of Lumberton.

L. D. raises only four types of pure-blooded peafowl: India blue, white, black shole and Java green. He won't mess with hybrids.

People from all over the country come to see and buy L. D.'s birds. The best time to see them is from March to July, the mating season, when the males are strutting. In July the males lose their beautiful tail feathers, and after that they slink around embarrassed and ashamed until the following spring.

"You've heard tell of proud as a peacock, ain't you?" L. D. said as one of his India peacocks spread its tail. "That's what he is. Proud. He's purty, ain't he? That's why I love to mess with them rascals."

PEMBROKE

Lost Colony Found?

The first attempt at a permanent English settlement in America ended in mystery. The settlers on Roanoke Island, near Manteo, disappeared, leaving only the word "Croatan" carved on a tree and became known as the Lost Colony.

Many Lumbee Indians believe the Lost Colony was never lost, that it simply joined with their ancestors and moved inland, the two groups eventually melding into one.

As evidence, they point to reports of early settlers along the Lumber River encountering native people with blue eyes and fair skin who spoke English words. As further proof, they point to the common Lumbee family names, Chavis, Dare, Lowry, Locklear and Oxendine— all also names of settlers in the Lost Colony.

Lumbees number more than 40,000 in Robeson County, perhaps 50,000 nationwide, and are the only Indians to hold onto their native lands without being forced onto a reservation. They make up perhaps a tenth of all American Indians, but have never been recognized as a tribe by the federal government.

In the '70s a resurgence of Indian pride swept through the Lumbees, and it is manifested in the Lumbee Homecoming on July 4th weekend each year. Lumbee beauty queens are chosen; a parade is held, and there are demonstrations of crafts and Indian dances.

From late June until August an outdoor drama, *Strike at the Wind*, about Lumbee hero Henry Berry Lowry, is presented Thursday-Saturday at the Lakeside Amphitheater at Riverside Country Club a

half mile off U.S. Highway 74 west of Pembroke. For more information
call Bruce Barton at (919) 521-0100.

RED SPRINGS

Flora MacDonald Highland Games

As a young woman in Scotland, Flora MacDonald became a heroine.
The Scots, led by Prince Charles, heir to the throne, were fighting the
English. They suffered a crushing defeat at Culloden Moor in April
1746, and Prince Charles retreated to the island of Benbecula, where he
was quickly surrounded and trapped. Flora came to the rescue by
disguising the prince in petticoat, dress and bonnet and leading him to
safety.

In 1774, Flora joined the emigration to this country and settled in
southeastern North Carolina, where she was welcomed by earlier
joining Scottish settlers. She soon became involved in the revolution,
with the Tories to oppose it.

Nevertheless, she has remained a heroine to Americans of Scottish descent, a great many of whom reside in southeastern N.C. A
college (now defunct) was named for her, and to continue her memory,
a non-profit group was formed in 1977 to sponsor the Flora MacDonald
Highland Games and Gathering of Clans.

Each year on the first weekend in October, several thousand
people gather to wear kilts and tartans, listen to the pipes and drums,
watch Scottish dances and traditional Highland athletic contests such
as the caber toss—pitching a 20-foot, 100-pound pole—and the sheaf
toss—throwing a sack of straw with a pitchfork.

The event is held in a field on State Road 1001, four miles north of
Red Springs, off N.C. Highway 71. For more information call G. T.
Ammons at (919) 843-4139.

SAMPSON

SPIVEY'S CORNER

National Hollerin' Contest

Ermon Godwin's granddaddy loved to holler.

"Most every man out in the country in those days did holler," Ermon says. "But some of them were better known for hollerin', and my grandfather, Bud Godwin, was a well known hollerin' man."

One day in 1969, Ermon, a banker in Dunn, asked John Thomas, a friend who worked at the local radio station, if he'd ever heard of the area's tradition of hollerin' as a means of communication in the days before telephones and easy transportation.

John thought he was kidding, so Ermon found a hollerin' man, George Demming, and got him to holler for him. John put George on the radio and after he hollered, remarked "We ought to have a hollerin' contest."

That was the beginning of the National Hollerin' Contest, one of the most popular of America's offbeat events, drawing more than 10,000 people annually to Spivey's Corner, a crossroads community on U.S. Highway 421, 11 miles south of Dunn.

The contest has attracted international attention, and many of the winners have appeared on Johnny Carson's Tonight Show.

Lots of screamers and yellers show up each year, but enough of the old timers to whom hollerin' was an art come to make it interesting.

But Dewey Jackson, an old timer who won the first contest in 1969, wonders how long the old hollerin' tradition can last at the contest.

"It's a lot of these here young'uns a-tryin' to holler," he says with contempt. "They ain't much hollerin' to it."

The hollerin' contest, held the first Saturday in June at Midway High School, includes a whistling contest, fox horn-blowing contest, conch-blowing contest, clogging, music and a barbecue. For more information, call Ermon Godwin at (919) 892-4133.

TURKEY

Claude Moore's Cabin Museum

Claude Moore is a former school principal, retired history professor, newspaper columnist and lecturer who enjoys few things more than dressing up in his Confederate general's uniform and leading people through his Cabin Museum.

Claude believes in making history tangible and throughout his life he collected pieces of it. In the late '50s, he bought a log cabin built in Duplin County in 1770 and moved it to Sampson County to house his collection. In 1977, he moved it again to its present location three miles north of Turkey (turn at Turkey's blinking light off N.C. Highway 24) on his great-grandfather's homeplace, where he now lives.

He also moved part of an 1859 plantation house to the site, restored it and opened both buildings as a museum. Thousands of items pertaining to the history of eastern North Carolina are on display, including turpentining equipment, barrel-making tools and many Confederate items. Claude is especially proud of an original Matthew Brady photograph of Robert E. Lee.

The museum may be seen free by appointment. Call Claude at (919) 533-3142.

SCOTLAND

LAURINBURG

Spaghetti's Grave

Forenzio Concippio, a carnival worker, got himself clobbered with a tent stake and killed in 1911. His father made a down payment on a funeral and told the undertaker he'd return with the remainder of the money and burial instructions. He didn't, and for the next 62 years, Forenzio's mummified body hung first on an embalming room wall, then in the garage at McDougald's Funeral Home in Laurinburg. The body, which became known as Spaghetti, because local people couldn't pronounce the proper name, became quite a tourist attraction, drawing people from all over the country.

In 1973, it drew the attention of a New York congressman of Italian ancestry who raised a storm of protest, and the funeral home finally buried Spaghetti in Hillside Cemetery on Hillside Street, just off U.S. Highway 401. The grave is on the right, beside the street, just past the cemetery entrance and bears a marker placed by the funeral home.

Dizzy Gillespie Jazz Hall of Fame

For the time being, it amounts to little more than a cap, a cape, a few other personal items, and some sketches and plans tacked on a conference room wall in the gymnasium of Laurinburg Institute, but Frank McDuffie Jr. has grand plans.

McDuffie now heads the black prep school started by his grandfather in 1904, the school from which famed jazz musician Dizzy Gillespie, a Cheraw, S.C. native, graduated in 1935. He has launched a plan to build by 1988 the John Birks (that's Dizzy's real name) Gillespie Center for Cultural Change and Jazz Hall of Fame on his campus.

The center will include an educational radio station, recording studios, a computerized jazz research center, a performing arts center, a museum of jazz recordings and memorabilia and a Hall of Fame honoring great jazz musicians.

If you should stop by to see Dizzy's cap and cape, also check the school's Sports Hall of Fame in the gym. The tiny school's alumni include Charlie Smith, the first black basketball player for the University of North Carolina; Sam Jones of the Boston Celtics; Jimmy Walker of the Detroit Pistons; Wes Covington, a major league baseball player; and Willie McCray of the San Francisco 49ers. The school is on McGirt Bridge Road, just off U.S. Highway 15–501. For more information call (919) 276-0684.

Indian Museum of Carolinas

Dr. David McLean was a missionary in Africa for 25 years before he returned to this country to teach anthropology at St. Andrews Presbyterian College in Laurinburg.

Once in North Carolina, he took an avid interest in the Indians who once had lived in the area. He began collecting Indian artifacts and came to be able to tell from any artifact which tribe had made it and in which period. He bought some artifacts, traded African artifacts for others, and some were given to him. As his collection grew over a period of 20 years, he began thinking of building a museum to house it. He opened it in 1968. The museum includes not only artifacts but dioramas showing how Indians of the Southeast lived.

Dr. McLean died in 1980, but his museum at 607 Turnpike Road may still be seen by appointment. Call Glenn Bingham at (919) 462-2321.

WAYNE

MT. OLIVE

Pickle Town, U.S.A.

All you have to do to find Mt. Olive, people from the town will tell you, is follow your nose. The whole town smells like pickles. It even calls itself Pickle Town, U.S.A.

Pickles are America's favorite preserved fruit or vegetable (there's debate about just which category cucumbers fall into). We each eat nearly nine pounds a year on the average. But nobody loves pickles more than the people of Mt. Olive. Pickles are the town's major industry.

In 1926, farmers around Mt. Olive found themselves with a cucumber crop they couldn't sell. Some enterprising businessmen in Mt. Olive built a large brine vat and stored the cucumbers in it until they could be sold to an out-of-state pickle packer. Within a few years, the businessmen were making their own pickles.

The Mt. Olive Pickle Co. is now one of the nation's largest, and because of it and the smaller Cates Pickle Co. in nearby Faison, North

Carolina and Michigan vie for the honor of being America's largest cucumber-growing state.

Eastern North Carolina farmers plant more than 30,000 acres in cucumbers, and each year the Mt. Olive Pickle Co. buys nearly 750,000 bushels and transforms them into some 25 million jars of pickles. At peak harvesting time in late June and July, cucumbers often come into the plant at the rate of 40,000 bushels a day.

The company makes nearly a third of the fresh cucumbers into pickles immediately. The rest are stored in a thousand huge redwood and cypress brine vats for year-round production.

Visitors may tour the plant Monday through Friday but are discouraged in peak harvesting time. They receive free pickle badges, balloons, bookmarks and other pickle paraphernalia, and lucky ones get to meet John Walker, the down-home, Harvard-educated company president, who drives a car with a license plate that reads DILLY-O, passes out pickle hats and t-shirts, and rattles off pickle jokes and puns with relish.

Drop-in visitors are welcome, but the company prefers that appointments be made with H. P. Stowe by calling (919) 658-2535. The plant, John Walker likes to say, is at Cucumber and Vine. Make that Witherington and Center.

THE
PIEDMONT

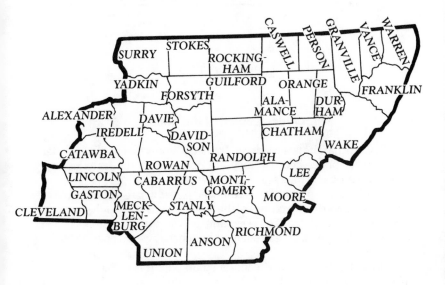

ALAMANCE

BURLINGTON

Outlet Capital of the South

North Carolina is a state filled with "outlets," stores that purport to offer much lower prices because they are operated by the factories that make the products they sell.

In the beginning, outlets were indeed places where factories sold to the public, often from a corner of the factory, and many such places do exist around the state. Their popularity was so great that stores began opening calling themselves outlets, although they weren't owned by the factories.

In some places, outlet centers sprang up. It is unlikely that any place has more outlets than Burlington, which boasts nearly 100, most in two large complexes alongside I-85. The town has even registered itself as the "Outlet Capital of the South." Tour buses bring shoppers to Burlington from throughout the country.

Other nearby towns also have outlets. Guides to all the outlets can be purchased at newsstands.

Wildlife Museum

The late Dr. Brodie McDade, a Burlington pediatrician, was a big-game hunter who traveled the world stalking his prey. He always returned with trophies.

When his collection of stuffed animals and mounted heads became too large for his home, he filled his clinic with them and delighted in showing them to children who frequently came in large groups to see them.

The collection eventually grew even too big for Dr. McDade's two-story clinic, and in 1956 he donated it to the town of Burlington for a museum. Money was raised to build a wing on the new administrative offices of the town's recreation department in City Park to house the collection. It became McDade Wildlife Museum.

The collection includes more than 500 different animals, large and small, all shot by Dr. McDade, who died in 1974. It is one of the largest such collections in the nation. Made up mostly of mounted heads, it also features horns, antlers, the tusks of a huge bull elephant, and many whole animals, including a crocodile, black bear, two leopards, a white tail deer and even bald and golden eagles.

The museum at 1333 Overbrook Road is open Monday–Friday, 8–5, at no charge.

SNOW CAMP

Robert Lindley's Studebaker Rest Home

Back in the days when a great many Southern men identified themselves with the kind of car they drove, Robert Lindley was a Studebaker man.

He just liked Studebakers and always drove one. After the Studebaker Company went out of business in 1966, he didn't see any need to quit driving the cars he loved. So just to be sure he'd always be able to drive one, he started collecting old Studebakers wherever he could find them, in whatever condition they happened to be.

He accumulated about 75 around his house in various states of repair, not to mention a few Henry Js and Willys. They enable Robert, a lifelong mechanic, to while away his days working on his beloved Studebakers in an old barn stocked full of Studebaker parts.

His Studebaker rest home is on Bethel Church Road.

ALEXANDER

HIDDENITE

World's Rarest Gemstones

New York mineralogist W. E. Hidden was looking for a source of platinum for inventor Thomas Edison when he came to Alexander County and discovered a pale green variety of the gem spodumene, which came to bear his name. Hiddenite is the world's rarest gem, found only on a few acres in Alexander County.

Those same acres also have borne some of the world's finest emeralds. Farmers who found emeralds while plowing in the 1800s called them green bolts and had little use for them.

Not until the 1960s when property owners began letting treasure hunters dig on their land did the gems of Hiddenite begin attracting national attention.

In 1969, a Lincolnton man, Michael Finger, found a 1,438-carat emerald, the largest ever found in North America.

In 1970, another digger found a large stone eight feet down and sold it to mine owner Lois Rist for $700. She later sold it to Tiffany and Co. in New York for $7,000. Cut and polished, the stone, called the Carolina Emerald, is now valued at $300,000.

Some of the most productive lands at Hiddenite have been bought by a large mining company and closed to the public. But Carolina Emerald Mines still has nearly four acres open for digging. The mine has a campground and showers and charges a daily fee for digging from sunup to sundown. It's on a gravel road off N.C. Highway 90 near Hiddenite School.

CABARRUS

CONCORD

A. B. Cook's Buffalo Ranch

A. B. Cook was a rodeo roper and trick rider, an old-time cowboy, who had a special fondness for buffaloes.

"I liked buffaloes," he once said, "because they were mean and getting extinct."

So after he settled on a ranch near Concord and started a meat-packing business, he got some buffaloes just to keep around. He had three shipped from Montana in 1952 and got six more from Colorado not long afterward. The herd eventually grew to about 40.

But A. B. was interested in more than just buffaloes. He bought many exotic breeds of cattle and goats, plus yaks, llamas, zebras, camels, lions, tigers, monkeys and other animals. He began to let people come to see them on Sunday afternoons, and eventually he had some stagecoaches built to carry visitors around the ranch. He even trained some goats to do a high-wire walk across a lake.

The high-wire goats haven't performed in recent years because they were visible from the highway and caused too many gawking drivers to have wrecks. But stagecoaches still make the 2 1/2-mile trip around the ranch for a small fee.

The ranch, on N.C. 49, one mile east of U.S. Highway 601, is open Easter through Labor Day, Tuesday–Saturday, 10–5:30; Sunday, 1–5:30. The rest of the year, it's open weekends only, weather permitting.

America's First Gold Mine

Conrad Reed was 12 when he found an unusual rock in Little Meadow Creek on his daddy's farm in 1799. It was beautiful, everybody agreed, and the family used it as a doorstop until John Reed took it to a jeweler in 1802. The jeweler realized the 17-pound rock was gold but didn't tell Reed. He bought it for $3.50. It was worth $3,500 at the time.

Reed later discovered he'd been cheated by the jeweler, demanded and got more money. Meanwhile word of the big nugget had spread. It created America's first gold rush.

John Reed panned only in the creek on his farm for gold in the beginning, but in 1825 it was discovered that the gold was coming from the white quartz so common in the area and Reed and some associates began digging into the creek banks. In 1831, they started digging America's first gold mine on the farm. So much gold was taken from mines in the area that the government opened a mint in Charlotte in 1837.

Reed died in 1845, before the California gold rush drew attention away from the North Carolina mines. His mine changed hands many times before it was finally closed in 1912.

In 1971, the 822-acre Reed farm was donated to the state and the old mine was restored and opened as a historic site in 1977. It attracts more than 100,000 visitors annually. A museum offers displays of old mining equipment and photos and maps of old mines.

A quarter mile of the hand-dug mine that goes 48 feet underground is open for visitors to examine, and the stamp mill used to crush ore from the mine has been restored.

Visitors may pan for gold from April through October, but the ore comes from Cotton Patch Mine, a commercial tourist mine in Stanly County.

The mine is on Reed Mine Road, two miles from N.C. Highway 200, four miles off U.S. Highway 601, about 14 miles south of Concord. It is open year-around, Monday–Saturday, 9-5; Sunday, 1-5; at no charge.

HARRISBURG

Tournament of Kings

What is the Tournament of Kings? Jousting perhaps? Guess again.

Try chain-saw racing.

It's called the Tournament of Kings because when it was started in 1978, the chain-saw company that sponsors it, Homelite, was advertising itself as the "Chain Saw King."

Some of the best loggers from around the world participate in the tournament. They gain entrance by winning one of 15 qualifying events held around the country each year.

The Tournament of Kings is the richest event in logging, offering $10,000 in prizes in addition to expense–paid trips to the event.

Contestants compete in six events—speed cutting, speed boring, precision cutting, tree felling, steeplechase and disc stacking.

In disc stacking, contestants have three minutes in which to cut ten slices as thin as possible off a 20-inch log. The shortest stack wins. The world record stack, set at this event, is an inch and three quarters. The world record for speed cutting, cutting three slices within a six-inch space off a 20-inch log, was also set at this event, 22.4 seconds.

The Tournament of Kings is held the first Wednesday in October at Charlotte Motor Speedway, qualifying day for the Miller 500 stock-car race. For information call John Thomas at (704) 588-3200.

Tournament of Kings, Canadian Ron Hartill competing

World's Longest Stock-car Race

Stock-car racing is the only major sport to come out of the South. From its beginnings in the '40s with moonshine liquor runners in souped-up cars racing each other on bets, the sport grew into a multi-million-dollar business and sophisticated racing cars running at high speeds on tracks called "superspeedways," attracting millions of spectators annually.

Stock-car racers were already running 500-mile races at Darlington when former moonshine runner Curtis Turner, one of the top stock-car racers, teamed with Charlotte businessman Bruton Smith in the late '50s and announced plans to build a mile-and-a-half track in Cabarrus County where they would hold a 600-mile race. Some in the sport believed that both cars and drivers were pushing their limits of endurance at 500-mile races, but the race went on anyway on an unfinished track in 1960.

It was called the World 600. It has remained the only 600-mile race, attracting more than 100,000 people to Charlotte Motor Speedway on U.S. Highway 29, near Harrisburg, north of Charlotte, each Memorial Day weekend.

CASWELL

HIGHTOWERS

Henry Warren's Shangri-la

Henry Warren was a wiry, industrious man who liked to add special touches to the things he did. He built his own house and when he added the sidewalk he imbedded in it, in many designs, more than 11,000 arrowheads he'd collected.

In 1969, when he was 77, Henry started another project. It came about because of another little special touch he'd added, a stone goldfish pond.

"I always wanted a water wheel for that pond," he told an interviewer. "Well, I got it. Then once I had it, I thought I'd build a mill house for it. You know, put it beside the pond and attach the wheel to it.

"I got all that and then I made a miller to turn the wheel. I hooked an electric motor up to the wheel, and it looks like the miller turning the wheel. Well, once I had that, I thought maybe the miller needed a home for his family. So I built that."

The miller's family, of course, needed a store and a church and a school and . . .

It just kept growing, all in miniature, a whole village built of white quartz Henry quarried on his farm. It was Henry's own little fantasy land, and appropriately he named it Shangri-la and opened it for all to enjoy. People came by the hundreds to wander through it and snap photographs.

"The kids are the ones who get the most involved in it," Henry said. "I just want them to enjoy it."

Henry kept expanding his village until his death at 85 in 1977. Before he died, he requested of his family that his Shangri-la be kept open to visitors. It's on N.C. Highway 86, east of Hightowers.

Henry Warren's Shangri-la

CATAWBA

CONOVER

North Carolina History in Jade

Richard Sipe loves rock. He has spent his working life as a rock mason. His hobby? He's a rockhound, of course.

On a rock hunt in 1972, when he was 44 years old, Richard dug a 7,000-pound mottled green nephrite jade boulder out of a North Carolina mountainside.

His first plan, once he got his monstrous find home, was simply to polish it and mount it on a pedestal next to his house.

In 1976, moved by the nation's bicentennial celebration, Richard decided to carve America's history into his boulder. A friend suggested that maybe he was being a little overly ambitious and should restrict himself to North Carolina's history. Richard agreed and he's been polishing and chipping away at his boulder with air-impact chisels ever since.

Next to his house, he erected a heated and lighted teepee-like tent over the boulder so he could work on it at night and in bad weather, and he's worked thousands of hours so far. His plan is to show the state's history along a road that begins in a tunnel of the distant past and winds around the rock into the infinity of the future.

Although he's never attempted sculpture before, Richard thinks he has a knack for it. "I have a pretty good eye," he says. "The rock dictates to me."

He hopes to finish the sculpture in 1986, but it could take longer. Meanwhile he invites visitors to see his progress. He usually works on it nights and weekends. His house is on County Home Road, three miles from N.C. Highway 16. For an appointment call (704) 464-0597.

HICKORY

World's Largest Arrowhead Collection

In 1940, Moon Mullins went to Georgia on vacation and found seven arrowheads. His wife, Irene, suggested collecting arrowheads might be a fun hobby.

"We started huntin' and we started buildin' and buildin' and buildin'," says Moon. "It's something got in me that I don't know. It'll grow on you and it'll hit you like that."

Through 20 states Moon and Irene hunted arrowheads—and they always found them.

"When I started this collection, if you'd told me, 'Moon, did you know that one day you'd have the largest collection of Indian arrowheads in the world?' I'd have said you were crazy. And now look at it.

World's largest arrowhead collection
Moon Mullins outside his museum

And I'm not braggin'. I don't know of anybody I would say as an individual in the world who has as big a collection as mine."

The collection numbers nearly half a million pieces, not only arrowheads but axes, tomahawks, hammers, stunners, spearheads, knives, fishhooks, gigs, needles, pestles, celts, pipes, idols and good luck charms, some dating back 20,000 years.

Over the years more than half a million people have come to see Moon's collection in an old building behind his house at 1228 Second Street, just off U.S. Highway 64 in Hickory. The building also houses a 64-seat movie theater with four professional projectors and a large collection of old movies that Moon also enjoys showing to visitors.

Moon's wife died in 1982, and he has lost both legs to circulatory problems, but he still hunts arrowheads and still finds them.

"Some people say ol' Moon can smell 'em," he says.

Moon's collection may be seen by appointment at no charge. Call (704) 327-5921.

Bernard's Waldensian Winery Museum

Waldensians who came to western North Carolina from Italy brought with them a tradition of wine making. About 1930, Mallie C. Bernard, who died in 1980, opened a commercial Waldensian winery in Icard, a Burke County town near the Caldwell County line.

A success from the beginning, the winery made popular wines from apples, peaches, strawberries and other fruits, as well as from native grapes. But its best seller was pokeberry, touted as a cure for rheumatism.

In 1948, Burke County voted against alcohol sales and forced the winery to close. More than 66,000 gallons of wine had to be turned to vinegar.

For the next 35 years, the winery and all its equipment sat idle. But in the fall of 1983, Mallie J. Bernard, who grew up working in his father's winery, joined with Leonard Bumgarner and Lorin Weaver to open Bernard's Waldensian Winery Museum in Hickory.

The museum includes much of the old equipment, including grape crushers, presses and 1,000-gallon redwood aging casks. The three men also revived Bernard's Waldensian Wines, having them made to old recipes under contract by another N.C. winery, and these wines are available for tasting in the museum. The new wines will include mountain huckleberry and sourwood honey, but there are no plans for reviving the once popular pokeberry.

The museum is in Kathryn's Cheese House on U.S. Highway 64 west, just a few miles from the winery's original location in nearby Icard. It is open 10–6 daily without charge.

TERRELL

Bill Abernathy's Rabbit Restaurant

When Bill Abernathy's hobby of raising show rabbits got out of hand, he began looking for something to do with all his rabbits. His Parkway Restaurant offered the solution. He put rabbit on the menu.

Acceptance was slow, but eventually the new dishes caught on and now the restaurant is the only one in the state where rabbit is the specialty of the house. Rabbit sausage is available for breakfast, fried rabbit, rabbit pie, rabbit salad, rabbit meatloaf and rabbit steak for lunch and dinner.

"People are finding out about rabbit," says Bill. "Rabbit is real low in cholesterol. It has practically none. It's higher in protein than beef and lower in fat than chicken. The sodium in it is so low that a diabetic could eat it."

It tastes—honestly—like chicken.

After you've finished your rabbit meal at the Parkway Restaurant, you can step into a corner of the dining room and buy a rabbit coat, muff, mittens and hat made from the pelts of the rabbits served earlier.

The restaurant is on N.C. Highway 150, near Lake Norman, about one mile east of N.C. Highway 16.

CHATHAM

BONSAL

North Carolina Railway Museum

In 1982, the East Carolina Chapter of the National Railway Historical Society raised $48,000 to buy a six-mile abandoned railroad spur near B. Everett Jordan Lake from Southern Railway.

To this spur, the club moved two locomotives, two flat cars, two boxcars, an old postal car, two old cabooses and several hand cars given to it over the years by different railroad companies. Restored by members, this equipment forms the nucleus of the New Hope Valley Railway, named for the original line that ran over the tracks from Bonsal to Durham.

This line, functioning only for the benefit of visitors, will be the centerpiece of the North Carolina Railway Museum the club plans to build in Bonsal as soon as money is available.

The equipment, meanwhile, can be seen on the tracks at Bonsal on State Road 1008.

SILER CITY

Milo Holt's Memory Mobile

It's a small trailer painted green. Milo Holt calls it his memory mobile. Inside, Bob Steele, Ken Maynard, Hoot Gibson and all the old movie cowboys still ride the range.

When Milo was growing up, those old cowboys reigned every Saturday at the Gem Theater in Siler City.

"We'd make a dime somehow and go to the show and spend Saturday afternoon watching the old cowboys," he remembers. "This was our biggest thrill for a whole week."

Milo never got over that thrill. He loved the old cowboys and even as a boy he collected photos of them and posters of their movies. Then in the mid-1950s when the old cowboy movies died out, he began renting films and showing them at home for friends. That led to collecting films, along with other memorabilia.

When the collection got to be too much for his house in 1970, Milo bought the old trailer and filled it. There several times a week and frequently on weekends he shows old cowboy movies to visitors and lets them view his collection, which includes a saddle once owned by silent movie star Fred Thompson.

In addition to the showings at the Memory Mobile, Milo regularly organizes larger gatherings of old cowboy movie buffs.

The Memory Mobile is about five miles east of Siler City on U.S. Highway 64 at Collins Pond. Cross the dam and turn right onto Memory Lane. Milo has no phone but is usually available nights and weekends.

Aunt Bea's House

Frances Bavier, a New York actress, appeared in movies and plays for 22 years without achieving great fame until 1960, when she landed a role as Aunt Bea in "The Andy Griffith Show" on CBS.

The show became number one in the ratings and won Frances Bavier an Emmy before it ended in 1970. It remains a top-rated rerun show.

In 1963, Frances Bavier came to North Carolina to undergo the famous rice diet at Duke University. While there she became friends with a Siler City woman who invited her to her home and took her on a tour around the state. It was Miss Bavier who urged "The Andry Griffith Show" writers to work Siler City into the story line of the show, which was set in North Carolina.

After her retirement from show business in 1972, Miss Bavier bought a large stone and brick house at 503 West Elk Street in Siler City and settled there. In her early years in the town, she made frequent public appearances in the area, but after her health began to fail, she went into seclusion. She does not receive visitors.

The Devil's Tramping Ground

It has been there for hundreds of years, a circular path in the woods, 40 feet in diameter, barren of growth.

It is one of North Carolina's best-known mysteries. Legend holds it is the place where the devil comes to tramp and brood and conjure evil in the darkness of night. Over the years, thousands of people have spent a scary night at the site, hoping to catch the devil at work. In the process, they have chopped down most of the trees for firewood and littered the privately owned site to the point of transforming it into a dump.

At one time the site was marked with a sign and even sported a picnic table for visitors but vandals destroyed them.

Scientific tests have proved that soil in the mysterious path is sterile, although the reason is unknown.

The Devil's Tramping Ground is about 10 miles south of Siler City on State Road 1100, about one mile north of N.C. Highway 902 at Harper's Crossroads. A gravel pull-off beside the road marks the site.

CLEVELAND

SHELBY

Hollywood East

It could be any other industrial complex. A low, white office building by the road, big warehouses down the hill, a sign that says "The EO Corp." The only indication that this might be something other than a typical industrial plant is a big chalet behind the office with statuary-lined pool, airstrip and garage with Rolls-Royce and airplane.

The chalet is home for movie mogul Earl Owensby, who has been called "the Cecil B. DeMille of the South," and "King of the Bs." The other buildings on the 112 rolling acres around the house make up the biggest movie studio outside of Hollywood, most efficient in the world, Earl Owensby likes to proclaim.

Earl Owensby was given away as a baby to a couple who later adopted him. He grew up in Cliffside, a small mill town in Rutherford County, where as a boy and young man he delivered newspapers, worked in the town movie theater and a cannery. He joined the marines, later became a tool salesman and eventually started his own tool company in Shelby.

But movies intrigued him—he is a devoted fan of *Gone With the Wind*—and in 1973 he decided to make one, strictly as a business venture.

"This was the only business the South didn't really have," he says. "It was just economics. It just had to work."

Owensby put a few hundred thousand dollars into an action- and violence-packed film called *Challenge*—starring Earl Owensby. It brought in $3 million, and Owensby decided he had found the right business and began building his studio.

The studio includes complete production facilities, with 100,000 square feet of soundproof studio space, underwater filming facilities and the largest cyclorama stage in the world. Here Owensby has turned out, among many others, such movies as *Death Driver, Wolfman, Living*

Legend and *Buckstone County Prison*—all starring Earl Owensby. None of his movies has ever lost money.

"There's nothing artistic about our movies," he admits. "They're commercial, you know, strictly commercial."

Independent producers have used the studio to make films that are more than commercial, through; one of them was the highly acclaimed *Reuben, Reuben.*

In the '80s, Owensby began making 3-D movies, and with new facilities to be added in 1984 his studio will become the most advanced 3-D movie studio in the world.

The studio, which is on Old Boiling Springs Road, off U.S. Highway 74 and N.C. Highway 150, offers tours on a limited group basis by appointment only, but never while films are in production. Call (704) 482-0611.

Hollywood East, Earl Owensby

Hollywood East, EO Studios

DAVIDSON

CHURCHLAND

Daniel Boone's Cave

Daniel Boone, the great frontiersman who cut the Wilderness Trail across the mountains into Tennessee and Kentucky, supposedly hid from Indians in a cave on a high hill overlooking the Yadkin River. The cave, with a two-foot opening and a ceiling height ranging from three to five feet, measures about 45 by 80 feet. It and 110 acres surrounding it are owned by the state and used as a park. A cabin where Boone once lived has been restored on the site.

The cave is off N.C. Highway 150 on State Road 1167, reachable by State Roads 1165 and 1162.

Boone's parents, Squire and Sarah Boone, are buried in Joppa Cemetery on N.C. Highway 601, a mile northwest of Mocksville in neighboring Davie County.

DENTON

Denton International Airport Fly-In, Old-Time Threshers Convention And Brown Loflin's Handy Dandy Railroad

As a boy, Brown Loflin would sit in school watching out the window enthralled as the steam locomotive made its regular run through Denton.

A born tinkerer, Brown was fascinated by anything mechanical. He was breaking down and rebuilding gasoline engines before he was 10. By 17, he was flying airplanes and building racing cars.

After prospering in business, Brown bought an 80-acre farm south of Denton and built a grass airstrip on it. In 1970, he and some other pilots gave airplane rides on July 4th weekend to raise money for the rescue squad. The event was so successful that it was held again the next summer, and the next. So many people came that the rescue squad started selling hot dogs and hamburgers.

"Somebody said, 'We ought to have an ol' timey wheat threshing dinner,'" Brown recalls. "I said, 'Why don't we just have a wheat threshing?'"

The next year, he bought and rebuilt an old steam threshing machine and the wheat threshing was added to the airplane rides. More steam devices came the following year and people began bringing their own steam engines to show off. Within a few years, the event had become the biggest steam show in the South. A steam sawmill, rock crusher, giant steam shovel, steamroller, even a functioning moonshine still were added to the show. In 1979, Brown bought his ultimate steam machine, a 50-ton H. K. Porter locomotive. By 1982, he had it restored and puffing around more than a mile of track laid out around the perimeter of his farm.

In addition to the steam devices, large numbers of antique gasoline and alcohol engines are displayed, powering everything from grist mills to clocks. The world's smallest steam-operated sawmill also can be seen.

The event lasts four days every July 4th weekend and includes music, dancing, military encampments and battle re-enactments, sky-diving shows and a huge flea market. Admission is charged. Brown's farm is off N.C. Highway 49 south of Denton. Signs mark the way. His Handy Dandy Railroad also operates on some other occasions during the year. For more information, call him at (704) 869-3663.

LEXINGTON

Barbecue Center of the Universe

It started in the '20s with tents pitched on a vacant lot across from the courthouse and pork shoulders cooking slowly over hickory coals in improvised cinder block pits. Sid Weaver and Varner Swicegood competed to sell barbecue trays and sandwiches to the crowds who came on court days.

That was the beginning of a whole school of North Carolina

barbecueing, now called Lexington-style, which became the dominant barbecue of the state's Piedmont.

North Carolina evolved two primary schools of barbecue: Eastern, in which whole pigs are cooked and served with white or yellow slaw, and Lexington, in which only shoulders are cooked and served with red slaw.

While Eastern barbecuers have largely turned to gas and electricity to cook their so-called barbecue, Lexington barbecuers have clung to tradition, cooking only over hickory coals as barbecue was meant to be cooked.

The tents across from the courthouse eventually became buildings. Warner Stamey bought out Varner Swicegood and spread Lexington barbecue to Greensboro. Sid Weaver was bought out by Allen Beck. Men who worked for Stamey and Beck went out on their own, opening barbecue houses in other nearby towns. But many remained in Lexington, and remarkably, the town has managed to support them. Lexington has more barbecue houses per capita than any place known—16 for a population of about 16,000—and all cook with wood.

They have made Lexington famous with barbecue fanciers, and that fame has spread worldwide. Lexington barbecuer Wayne Monk of Lexington Barbecue #1 was summoned to cook for international leaders at the Williamsburg Summit Conference in 1983.

Lexington, however, has never made much of a to-do about its barbecue, not even bothering to erect a sign recognizing it, but that may be about to change. In 1983, the town council voted to begin holding an annual Barbecue Festival on the third weekend in October, 1984.

Original Golden Berry Holly

It was just a freak of nature, a holly tree that sprouted yellow berries instead of red. Matthew Morgan found it growing in a pasture on his father's farm in Rowan County and moved it to his front yard in Lexington at 20 Morgan Drive. That was where Minnie Darr, a local holly enthusiast, saw it.

Minnie took clippings from the tree to a Holly Society of America convention in 1959 and created a sensation. Officially registered as a new variety of holly, the Morgan Gold, the tree gained worldwide fame. Offspring from it, created by grafting cuttings from the tree, grow in the National Arboretum and in Britain's Royal Gardens.

THOMASVILLE

World's Largest Duncan Phyfe Chair

One day in 1921, Charles Sturkey, managing editor of the weekly *Chair Town News*, got to boasting to a fellow newspaperman from another town about how many chairs were made in Thomasville's several furniture factories. He pointed out that enough chairs were produced in the town to allow every resident to sit in a new one every day. In his enthusiasm, he got carried away and went on to tell how Thomasville was going to build the largest chair in the world to note its eminence in chair building.

There was no such plan, and the editor was taken aback a few days later when a story about the big chair appeared in his friend's newspaper and requests for more information began coming in.

To save face, Sturkey talked the town fathers into building such a chair and in 1922, Thomasville Chair Co. (later to become Thomasville Furniture Industries) assigned four men to the task.

The chair was built at the company's Plant C and contained enough lumber to build 100 ordinary dining-room chairs.

"We made it out of forest pine," one of the workers, Walter Loftin, would recall years later, "the best wood we had. We had to build it in what was the bending room, because that was the only department which had a big enough door so we could get the chair out."

The chair was 13.5 feet tall and was upholstered with leather from the hide of a single Swiss steer. It was erected in the heart of town alongside the mainline Southern Railway tracks so passengers in passing trains could see it.

Gradually, the chair decayed and in the mid-1930s, it was dismantled. But people in town had grown accustomed to the big chair and they kept talking about what a shame it was that they didn't have it any more.

Finally, in 1948, the Chamber of Commerce and the chair company agreed to build a new one that would last. The Duncan Phyfe design was chosen and local sculptor James Harvey set about building the chair of steel and concrete. The 12-foot-tall limestone base was anchored eight feet deep. The chair rose 18 feet above the base, and solid brass rods were used in its lyre back.

Dedicated in 1951, the chair remains the town's centerpiece at the corner of Randolph and Main streets. Several Misses America and President Lyndon B. Johnson have climbed into the chair to pose for pictures.

World's largest Duncan Phyfe chair

DURHAM

DURHAM

Pharmacy Museum

Elsie Booker is a pharmacist who is fascinated by old things. Soon after her graduation from pharmacy school in 1945, she did some relief work in old-time drug stores and became intrigued with some of the old tonics and potions she saw on the shelves. She started collecting them.

Her husband, John, a tobacco company employee, collected tobacco paraphernalia, and together they began scouring the country, adding to their collections. In the process, they picked up a lot of other items from old stores, and in 1973 they decided to make use of them by opening Patterson's Mill Country Store on Fearington Road, off N.C. Highway 54 between Raleigh, Durham and Chapel Hill. The store is a replica of an old-time store, furnished with what has been described as one of the nation's best collections of mercantile Americana. It offers North Carolina hand-crafted items for sale.

In 1974, the Bookers built a wing on the store to house Elsie's extensive collection of old-time pharmaceuticals, more than 10,000 patent medicines, pills, tonics and potions, some dating back to 1880, along with pharmacy equipment. The wing is a replica of a turn-of-the-century pharmacy. Adjoining it is an old-time doctor's office. Visitors may browse through both at no charge.

Elsie's collection has been recognized by the American Institute of the History of Pharmacy, as well as by the Smithsonian Institution as one of America's finest.

"Smithsonian says it far surpasses theirs," says Elsie.

The store is open Monday–Saturday, 10–5:30; Sunday, 2–5:30.

The Tobacco Museum

At the end of the Civil War, an Orange County tobacco farmer named Washington Duke walked home from the war to find that most of his goods had been pilfered except for a 25-pound sack of tobacco he had carefully hidden.

He toasted the tobacco, spread it over a corncrib floor, and he and his three sons beat it with sticks until it was shredded enough to be smoked. This he packaged and sold. Thus was the beginning of the world's largest tobacco company.

Soon Duke began processing tobacco in an old barn. Then he built a two-story factory, one room upstairs, one down, near his house. By 1874, W. Duke & Sons Tobacco Co. had moved into downtown Durham to compete against the W. T. Blackwell Tobacco Co., makers of the popular Bull Durham Tobacco.

Ten years later, a cigarette machine was perfected and Duke managed to get sole rights to it. With these machines, Washington Duke's youngest son, James Buchanan, went to New York and started a factory that soon gobbled up all the other major tobacco companies. From 1890 to 1911, when the government forced its breakup, Duke's American Tobacco Company was the world's largest.

James Buchanan Duke went on to become a tycoon, moving into aluminum, railroads, textiles and electrical power (he founded Duke Power Co.). In 1924, he gave $40 million to Trinity College to establish Duke University.

The old Duke homeplace was owned by the university until 1974 when it was given to the state. Three years later, it was opened as a state historic site and tobacco museum. Tobacco equipment and paraphernalia may be seen, along with a 22-minute film detailing the story of tobacco. The house, the corncrib where Duke started his company, and the two-story factory may be toured.

Each year on the last weekend in July, a tobacco barn party is held to demonstrate how tobacco once was tied on sticks and hung in mud-chinked log barns to be cured with wood fires. The party includes roasting corn and making hoecakes in the curing fire ashes.

On the first Sunday in October a mock tobacco auction is held at the museum, featuring professional auctioneers, including the winner of the tobacco auctioneering world championships held in Danville, Virginia.

The museum, at 2828 Duke Homestead Road, is open 9-5 daily, 1-5 Sunday, without charge.

Tying tobacco at Tobacco Museum

Mock auction at Tobacco Museum
Photo: Jim Thornton

*Corn crib where Washington Duke started world's largest
tobacco company, at tobacco museum*

FORSYTH

KERNERSVILLE

Korner's Folly

Jule Korner was the grandson of Joseph Korner who founded Kernersville. With his inheritance he invested successfully in real estate, allow-

ing him to pursue his other interests, art and interior decorating. But it was his genius for advertising that brought him fame.

Using the name Ruben Rink, he made Bull Durham tobacco world famous in the last century. He created and painted the roll–your–own tobacco's bull symbol on barns across the nation—even on the Rock of Gibraltar and the pyramids of Egypt.

His fortune amassed, he returned to Kernersville to design and build his dream house, an ornate, eclectic house of 22 rooms on seven levels. A passing farmer, observing the construction of the peculiar house, was heard to remark, "That will surely be Jules Korner's Folly." Hearing of it, Korner had "Korner's Folly" inlaid in tile across the main entrance.

Korner was a bachelor when he started the house in 1878. He expanded and remodeled it eight years later when he married. The house includes a ballroom with statuary and ornate wood carvings. An upper floor offers a little theater with murals and frescoes in the ceiling. On the front porch is a small fireplace called "The Witches Corner," provided to keep witches out of the house. One room in the home was designed to be fireproof. Built of tile and marble, it was called the smoker and was the only room in the house where Korner, a non-tobacco user, allowed smoking.

Korner's Folly remained in the Korner family until it was bought and restored by a non-profit foundation in 1970. It is open Sundays, 1–5, for a fee. For information, call (919) 993-4134.

WINSTON-SALEM

North Carolina's
Most Productive Cigarette Plant

Once the largest cigarette plant in the world, R. J. Reynolds's Whitaker Park Plant is now third in size behind Phillip Morris plants in Richmond, Virginia, and Cabarrus County. But it remains the most productive in the state (and second-most in the world), turning out nearly half of Reynolds's annual output of 200 billion cigarettes.

The plant has 40 cigarette-making machines, each with a capacity of 7,000 cigarettes a minute. It's the only plant that takes visitors on guided tours into the production area.

Open to visitors Monday–Friday, 8 a.m.–10 p.m., the plant also has a display area that tells the history of tobacco and includes exhibits of tobacco paraphernalia such as old advertisements, tobacco packs, tins, and even recordings of old radio shows sponsored by the company's cigarettes. It's on Reynolds Boulevard, off Akron Drive, off U.S. Highway 52 North.

South's Largest Chess Tournament

Little tournament chess was being played in the South when Alan Lipkin, a Winston-Salem chess buff and chemistry professor, decided that was a shame. He wanted to start a tournament, but lacked the cash to front the prize money. So he talked a fellow chess player, Lawrence G. Pfefferkorn, a mortgage banker, now dead, into putting up the money and thus was born the Lawrence G. Pfefferkorn Chess Tournament in 1974. It has been played annually since and now attracts more than 200 entrants, including many of America's chess masters.

"There's nothing like this tournament in the South," says Lipkin. "It's a monster."

The tournament is played the last weekend in July at the Winston-Salem Hilton.

World's Largest Painting

In 1880, French historical artist, Paul Philippoteaux, painter of many cycloramas, came to the United States and undertook what he called "the greatest effort of my life"—a cyclorama of the climax of the Civil War Battle of Gettysburg on July 3, 1863.

It took Philippoteaux and 16 assistants two and a half years to finish it. The painting was put on display in Chicago in 1883 and in the first year attracted nearly half a million people, who paid nearly $250,000 to see it.

The painting eventually passed into the hands of Emmett McConnell of Hollywood, who owned and exhibited many such cycloramas. He last exhibited it in 1932. For the next 30 years, the painting remained stored in a Chicago warehouse.

In 1964, Winston-Salem painter Joe King, who was commissioned to do portraits of President Richard Nixon, Queen Elizabeth and the royalty of Saudi Arabia, bought the painting as a curiosity. Since then he has kept it in a warehouse in Winston-Salem, unavailable to the public.

Joe says he would like to change that and put the painting on view, but he has no definite plans to do so. It would take quite a building to display it. The painting is 70 feet tall—the height of a seven-story building—and 410 feet long. It is recognized by the Guiness Book of World Records as the largest in the world.

World's Largest Coffee Pot

When customers complained to Julius Mickey that they had trouble finding the tin shop he and his brother Samuel operated on Main Street in Salem, an early Moravian community, Julius was quoted as saying, "I'll put up a sign that will tell everybody where I am and where I do business."

That he did. On a pole in front of his shop, he and his brother built a coffee pot 16 feet in circumference and more than 12 feet tall. That was in 1858.

Why the brothers chose a coffee pot for a symbol isn't known, but coffee pots were considered necessities in those days and the tin shop was across the street from a public camping ground and coffee pots dangled from the sides of all the wagons of travelers who gathered there.

No matter why they chose it, the coffee pot was a success. Its fame spread widely, and eventually it became a symbol for Salem itself.

It stood in the same spot for a century, but construction of Interstate Highway 240 caused it to be moved, first to a temporary location, later to its present spot on the north side of the Old Salem restoration at Main Street and the Salem bypass.

FRANKLIN

LOUISBURG

National Whistling Convention
And World's Largest Collection
of Recorded Whistling Music

In 1974 at a folk festival on the campus of Louisburg College, a singer decided to whistle his tune instead of singing it. The crowd loved it, and at the next year's festival a small whistling contest was held under a big oak tree on the campus.

The contest grew every year until the folk festival was overwhelmed and forgotten. By 1981, the contest had become the National Whistling Convention, bringing some of the world's most famous whistlers to Franklin County Courthouse on the third weekend each April.

Professional whistlers perform concerts of popular and classical music, but the highlight of the day is the whistling contest. Competitors come from all over the country and employ many whistling styles. There are pucker whistlers, teeth whistlers, tongue whistlers and finger whistlers of many varieties.

Awards are given for youngest and oldest whistler, for popular music and classical, for special sounds and loud whistling (111 decibels took the award in 1983), and a national champion whistler is named.

During the convention, the National Whistling Museum is open in an old store building across from the courthouse. The museum houses whistling memorabilia and the world's largest collection of recorded whistling music. During the convention, the museum also displays the world's largest collection of whistles, owned by Carlin N. Morton of Ft. Myers Beach, Florida. The museum may be seen by appointment throughout the year. For information about the museum or the convention, write Allen de Hart, Louisburg College, Box 845, Louisburg, N.C. 27549, or call (919) 496-2521.

GASTON

CHERRYVILLE

America's Only Trucking Museum

When Grier Beam was growing up on a farm near Cherryville, he was mainly interested in chickens. He loved working with them, but he had to do other farm chores, too, as well as working at his father's sawmill and cotton gin.

When he went away to college at N.C. State, he studied poultry science and got a degree in it in 1931. He immediately landed a job with a poultry co-op in Florida. Soon afterwards, the price of eggs dropped, and the co-op folded.

The Depression was on and Beam was unable to find a job, so he returned home, bought a used '31 Chevrolet truck for $360 on credit, and began hauling coal to the county schools and making regular runs to Florida to bring back oranges and vegetables.

From that small beginning grew Carolina Freight Carriers, the largest trucking company in North Carolina, tenth largest in the nation. It has more than 5,000 employees and hauls freight all over North America and Europe.

Over the years, Beam kept a lot of the old trucks that his company phased out and made a hobby of restoring them. But he never was able to find a '31 Chevrolet like the one he used to start his company. When he finally did find one, he decided to open a trucking museum with it as the featured attraction.

To house his collection of trucks, he built a building on Mountain Street in Cherryville, next to the old gas station in which he once had used a corner as his first office. He opened the museum in the fall of 1982 with 14 trucks and displays about the trucking business. The museum charges no admission and is open Friday and Saturday, 10-5; Sunday, 1-5.

New Year's Shoot-In

On New Year's Day, you might say that Cherryville is a booming town.

For more than 150 years, townspeople have followed a tradition started by the town's German settlers, who believed that bad luck and witches could be driven away by welcoming a new year with black powder explosions.

On New Year's Day, dozens of residents armed with old muskets and plenty of black powder go from house to house and business to business in the town. At each stop they recite an old sing-song chant designed to bring good luck, then one by one discharge their muskets with resounding booms. The annual ritual usually takes all day to complete. When New Year's Day falls on Sunday, it is held on January 2.

DELLVIEW

America's Smallest Town

At one time every family in Dellview owned a Dodge and the Chrysler Company was so impressed that it wrote a story about the town in its company magazine. Didn't matter that there were only two families in town.

Dellview was incorporated in 1924, so the story goes, because brothers A. T. and J. Henry Dellinger wanted to give themselves authority to shoot stray dogs that threatened their chicken business. Of course, some say it was because Duke Power Company would only extend its lines to incorporated areas.

The town was incorporated in a square with each side 1,500 feet long. The only brick structure in town, a chicken incubator, sat at its exact center.

Deaths brought the town's population to one at one point, Mrs. J. Henry Dellinger, who elected herself mayor and town board and then named herself police chief, but by the 1980 census, population had risen to eight. Dellview is on N.C. Highway 150 on the western edge of Cherryville.

GASTONIA

Starving Artist Festival

When the *Gastonia Gazette* began looking around for a public service project in 1970, the newspaper decided to do something to promote art. How better to promote it than by giving artists a chance to make a little money?

So the paper started the Starving Artist Festival to allow artists and craftsmen a chance to display and sell their works. About 50 exhibitors participated in the first event. More than 200 now take part, and as many as 50,000 people have come to see their works on the second Sunday in September in the newspaper parking lot at 2500 Wilkinson Boulevard. For information call (704) 864-3291.

McADENVILLE

Christmas Town

In 1956, the McAdenville Men's Club decorated some trees around the town's community center for Christmas. They used red, green and white lights, and the reception was so good that they decorated a few more trees the next year.

Now the town decorates some 250 trees with more than 300,000 lights. A lake in the center of town serves as a reflecting pool for 75 of the trees, and colored lights also play on a fountain in the lake.

Decorating of the town begins in September. In addition to the lighted trees, homes in the town are decorated elaborately. A traditional yule log parade is held, and a 30-foot bell tower chimes carols for visitors nightly.

There are visitors aplenty. Nearly a quarter million vehicles pass through the town in December bringing people to see the decorations. The lights glow Monday–Friday, 5–9; Saturday and Sunday, 5–10; December 2-26.

GUILFORD

GREENSBORO

African Heritage Museum

Mattye Reed spent 12 years in Africa while her husband, William, was a diplomat for the Agency for International Development. During that time, she collected hundreds of African art objects. After she and her husband returned to this country and her husband became director of international affairs at predominantly black A&T State University, Mrs. Reed donated her collection to the African Heritage Center students had started on the campus in the late '60s.

She cleaned and refurbished a campus house to display the collection and opened it as the African Heritage Museum in 1974. Since then, several major African collections have been donated to the museum, which now features more than 3,000 items from 22 African nations and the Caribbean. Included are fabrics, baskets, carvings, books, busts of African kings and queens, weapons, ceremonial drums, masks and many other items. The collection is recognized as one of the nation's finest exhibits of African art. The museum, on Nocho Street on the A&T campus, is open 9–5, Monday–Friday, at no charge. Weekend tours may be arranged by calling Mattye Reed at (919) 379-7874.

Herman Mesimore's Tumbling Pigeon Show

Over the years, Herman Mesimore has raised many varieties of pigeons in his back yard at 1215 Gregory Street. He has cut back some and now keeps only about 250 pigeons of 17 breeds. Herman's specialty is acrobatic pigeons, the ones called rollers.

These pigeons, bred since 1735, fly high into the air, suddenly roll over into a tailspin and tumble toward earth. Usually, they pull out just in the nick of time and resume flight. Sometimes they don't and die.

Herman's favorites are the parlor rollers, birds incapable of flight that do tumbling routines on the ground.

"One guy told me, 'I had a girlfriend that would do that every time I tried to put my arm around her,'" Herman said, as he watched one of his pigeons flopping away from him.

For years, Herman has put on free pigeon shows in his back yard on weekday mornings for school groups, Scout troops and others. Shows can be arranged by appointment. Call (919) 273-1842.

Shorty LaRose's Clock Museum

Shorty LaRose spent a working lifetime selling parts for watches and clocks, but it wasn't until 1974, when he was past retirement age that he bought his first old clock.

That was a "cottage clock" made in 1885 and Shorty paid $35 for it. It also was the beginning of what would become one of America's great collections of American-made clocks. Shorty now has more than 850 clocks, some of them among the rarest on earth. He has grandfather clocks, table clocks, wall clocks, kitchen clocks, employee time clocks, bank vault clocks, cuckoo clocks, even a hickory-dickory-dock clock with a mouse that runs to the top.

All of his clocks are on display at the Greensboro Clock Museum at Commerce Place and Bellemeade Street in downtown Greensboro (it's the place with the big clock out front). The museum is open weekdays, 9–5. A small admission is charged.

Lunch Counter Where Sit-Ins Began

Late in the afternoon of February 1, 1960, four students from Greensboro's all-black N.C. A&T College—David Richmond, Franklin McCain, Ezell Blair and Joseph McNeill—walked into the F.W. Woolworth store on South Elm Street and took seats at the lunch counter.

Denied service and asked to leave, they remained seated, prompting the store manager to close the store early. The four left quietly, but the following day a larger group of students appeared and took seats in protest of segregated facilities. Within two months, the sit-ins, as they became called, spread to 54 cities in nine states and eventually toppled segregationist policies.

Twenty years later, the four students who started the protests returned to the lunch counter together for the first time since their historic action. This time they came to be honored by the city. They were served breakfast but were unable to eat it because of the attentions of so many reporters, photographers and onlookers.

The lunch counter is still open.

HIGH POINT

East's Biggest Drag Boat Races

From a small beginning in 1974, the Oak Hollow Drag Boat Races became the premiere event of its type in eastern America, attracting the world's best boat drag racers and fastest boats.

More than 100 boats compete in three hull classes—jet, flat and hydro—over a quarter-mile course. Some boats reach speeds of more than 200 m.p.h.

The world speed record of 215.82 m.p.h. was set at the event by Eddie Hill in 1982, the same year racer Jimmy Wright died in a spectacular crash during the races.

Thousands of spectators are drawn to the two-day races sponsored by the High Point Jaycees on the last weekend in July at Oak Hollow Reservoir off Eastchester Drive (N.C. Highway 68) in north High Point.

World's Largest Bureau

High Point calls itself the Furniture City and with good reason. Not only is it a center of furniture manufacturing, it is the site of the world's largest furniture show, attracting thousands of furniture store buyers from all over the world each spring and fall.

For more than half a century, the city's symbol of its prominence in the furniture field has been the world's largest bureau. Built in 1926, four years after neighboring Thomasville (which calls itself the Chair City) created the world's biggest chair, the big bureau was designed to share in the publicity Thomasville was attracting. But the bureau also had a practical purpose. It became a visitor center and office for the Chamber of Commerce, which built it.

A frame structure 27 feet long, 14 feet wide and 32 feet high, the bureau was designed to look as if it had four drawers. A large sign on top gave the appearance of a mirror. The entrance was on the side.

Originally built in Tate Park on North Main Street, the bureau was given to the High Point Jaycees and moved to 508 North Hamilton Street in 1951. The Jaycees installed a basement and later added another room to the back, and the bureau remains the club's offices.

Visitors frequently come to see the bureau and want to look inside. "Particularly children," former Jaycee secretary Katherine Nibbelink was once quoted as saying. "They would come in and ask to see my drawers."

World's largest bureau

OAK RIDGE

America's Oldest Continuously Operating Water Mill

It has had many names, most recently Bailes Mill, but generally it has just been called the Old Mill. Built by Nathan Dillon on Beaver Creek about 1745, the mill was captured by British troops before the Battle of Guilford Courthouse during the Revolutionary War.

In 1822 owner Joel Sanders built a larger mill, the current one, downstream from the dam. A succession of owners kept the mill operating with only brief interruptions until 1975 when miller Lloyd Lucas died, making it the oldest water mill in the country in continuous operation. The mill stood idle until 1977 when it was bought by Englishman Charlie Parnell, who still operates it.

"The bloody British are back," Parnell joked after buying it.

Open daily, 6 a.m.–9 p.m., the mill is on N.C. Highway 68, south of Oak Ridge.

IREDELL

BARIUM SPRINGS

Little Joe's Church

In September, 1901, a 6-year-old boy, Joe Gilland, and his 7-year-old sister, Janie, were brought to Barium Springs Home for Children. The orphanage had no church, and the children had to climb aboard wagons to attend church in the nearby town of Troutman.

Joe didn't care for that travel and announced one day that when he became a man he was going to build a church at the orphanage. A church with a porch. He was adamant about the porch.

Early in the winter of 1904, Joe fell ill and died. Under his pillow was found an old purse with 45 cents in it, pennies he'd saved to build his church.

When word spread of Joe's death and his unfulfilled dream, money began coming to the orphanage from all over the state to build Joe's church. Two years after his death, enough had come to start building. A year later, a little white church was completed. It had a porch and was named Little Joe's Presbyterian Church.

In 1955, an imposing new brick church was built on the children's home grounds alongside U.S. Highway 21. It has a high steeple, stained windows, chimes and a wide porch with massive white columns.

A couple of hundred feet away in a small, shaded cemetery is a flat concrete marker over the grave of Joe Gilland. It's behind the church. The porch can't be seen from there.

Joe Gilland's grave behind Little Joe's church

LOVE VALLEY

Home of the Man
With the World's Strongest Teeth

In 1970, Joe Ponder, a long-distance truck driver, broke his neck in a traffic accident. He spent a lot of time in traction recuperating. One day while lying in bed looking at a rafter above him, he wondered if he could throw a sheet across the rafter and pull himself up with his teeth. He tried it and found that he could.

Joe began amusing himself by hanging from the rafter by his teeth. After he recovered, he went looking for other things he could do with his teeth. He started pulling a pickup truck with his teeth, moved up to his tractor trailer, then graduated to a boxcar. He bent a steel bar with his teeth and next thing anybody knew, he was flying around dangling beneath a helicopter, hanging on by the skin of his teeth.

As Joe's fame spread, he was invited to Circleville, Ohio, to lift the world's largest pumpkin, 343 pounds, with his teeth. He went on to Naked City, Indiana, where he lifted two naked women with his teeth. Later, Joe lifted a caged panther and a mule with his teeth.

Joe has also fired the world's fastest machine gun—2,000 rounds a minute—with his teeth, and he had a special set of golf clubs made so he can play golf with his teeth. He can chip and putt okay, but has yet to hit an acceptable drive.

"Just can't get any lift on the ball," he says.

In 1978, while putting on a free show at his house, Joe attempted a "death slide" along a cable into his back yard swimming pool, hanging on by his teeth. His mouthpiece broke, and Joe fell 25 feet to the ground, breaking 27 bones. Fortunately, his teeth weren't hurt.

Joe, who is available for paid performances, still puts on periodic free shows at his home, which adjoins the leather company he operates on Main Street. For information, call Joe at (704) 592-2010.

The East's Only Working Western Town

No motorized vehicles are allowed on Love Valley's Main Street, only horses. This street looks like a set for an old western movie. That's exactly how Andy Barker wanted it.

"This is a horse and cowboy town," he says. "Everybody in town wears western clothes."

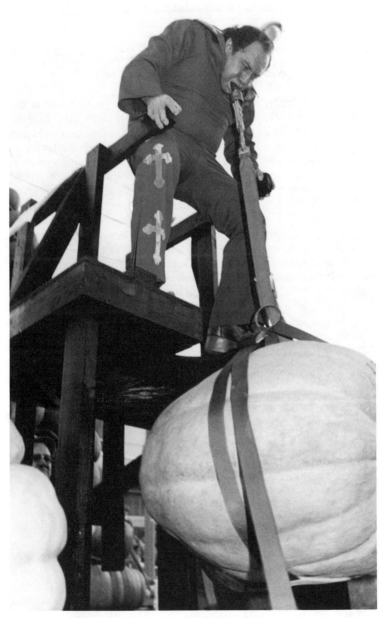

Joe Ponder lifts world's largest pumpkin with his teeth

Joe Ponder lifts mule with his teeth

Andy always liked horses, and while he was away fighting in World War II, the idea came to him to build a western-style resort town when he got back home—if he did.

He did come back, went into the construction business with his father in Charlotte, prospered, and in 1954, he acquired a tract of land in the Brushy Mountains of northwestern Iredell County and began building his town.

Now incorporated, Love Valley has a mayor—Andy—and a town council. It's the only town in the East with a marshal, Ed McCoy. It has a hotel, a saloon and a dance hall. The sidewalks are wood, and hitching posts and water troughs line the unpaved Main Street. The town once had a jail, but it was closed by federal inspectors.

"Told me if I opened it back up, they'd lock me up—and not in my own jail," says the mayor, who has twice been a candidate for governor.

Numerous rodeos and other horse-related events are staged annually at Love Valley. "We have something every weekend during the

Main Street, the East's only Western town

summer," says Andy. There's no admission fee to the town or riding trails, and camping is available.

"This is not a tourist trap," says the mayor. "People are always asking, 'What's the gimmick?' They think there's got to be a gimmick, but there's not."

The Love Valley Road is 12 miles north of Interstate Highway 40, off N.C. Highway 115. For more information write Andy at Box 607, Love Valley, 28677, or call (704) 592-7451.

STATESVILLE

America's Oldest Hot Air Balloon Rally

Tracy Barnes, who in 1958 becamethe first person to fly a hot air balloon across the United States; designed and perfected several new safety features on the balloons he flew, and other balloonists began asking him to make balloons for them.

So in 1973, he settled in Iredell County, where rents were cheap, and began making balloons in an old chicken house.

The following year in October he held a rally to give the people for whom he was making balloons a chance to get together, get to know one another and fly their balloons over the Iredell hills while the leaves were in fall splendor.

The Balloon Works, Tracy called his company, and it kept growing until it occupied four chicken houses and hit peak production of 300 balloons a year in 1979. Tracy sold the company in 1983, and it moved into a new plant in Statesville.

As the company grew, so did the annual get-together for customers. It evolved into the National Balloon Rally, one of the largest and most colorful spectacles of its kind. Once held in a pasture next to the chicken houses, the two-day event on the third weekend in October is now held at the Statesville Airport south of Interstate Highway 40 off Amity Hill Road.

In 1983, 85 balloons were in the air at the same time, and as many as 15,000 people came to watch. Balloonists compete in a hare and hound chase and attempt to win a new car by snagging the keys to it from a tall pole (somebody did it for the first time in 1983). They also try to win bowlsful of diamonds by tossing three-ounce sacks of grits into the bowls from 100 feet.

An air show, sky diving and music are also part of the rally, and spectators may pay to take balloon rides.

World's Second-Largest
Gone with the Wind Collection

Bill Wooten was already a confirmed movie addict when as a teen-ager he went with his family to see *Gone with the Wind* when it came out in 1939.

He loved movies. He'd been going to movies alone since he was 9. He remembers having his mother write a note asking that he be excused from school because of pink eye, then spending the whole day in a theater watching *King Kong*.

But no movie before or since touched him like *Gone with the Wind*. It captivated him; enchanted him.

"It seemed to be the complete entertainment," he says. "Everything in it was perfection."

Bill is embarrassed to tell how many times he's seen the movie. Begin guessing around 100. When he wasn't watching the movie, chances are he was collecting items pertaining to it. His collection of newspaper and magazine clippings about the movie, still photos from it, posters and other advertising materials, books, sound track albums and other items is second only to that owned by fellow collector Herb Bridges, a Georgian. Bill even has an original press book distributed before the movie came out. "So rare," he says, "that even David O. Selznick Studios doesn't have it."

Bill, a librarian and former radio announcer who began his collection while working in a Charlotte theater as a student at Davidson College, will show it by appointment. Call (704) 873-8835.

LINCOLN

LINCOLNTON

George Fawcett's
UFO Museum and Convention

George Fawcett was 10 when he started a World War II scrapbook that grew to 48 volumes. It was while he was collecting material for his scrapbooks that he first came across a report of American pilots seeing strange objects in the sky over Germany. In 1947, when a pilot reported seeing unidentified flying objects over Mt. Ranier in Washington, thus sparking the UFO era, George was fascinated. He has remained passionately fascinated since.

A former YMCA director now in newspaper advertising, George has devoted much of his life to tracking down UFOs and proving their existence. He has collected and read more than 500 books on the subject and written one of his own. He has personally investigated thousands of reported sightings, gathered thousands more reports and documents, including previously classified reports of government investigations, and collected 800 photos of UFOs, plus models of UFOs and sculptures of alien creatures reported seen by witnesses he has interrogated.

The material overflows his house and garage at 602 Battleground Road. "It's godawful," he says. "It's all over the place."

For years, George has dreamed of establishing a UFO museum and study center to house his collection. But for now he makes do with exhibits in the UFO Room at his wife Shirley's Super Sub Sandwich Shop at 333 E. Main Street.

George, who lectures widely on UFOs and even teaches a credit college course on the subject, also organizes a UFO convention held each June on Father's Day weekend at the Nature Science Center in Winston-Salem.

For information, write George at 602 Battleground Avenue, Lincolnton 28092, or call (704) 735-5725.

MECKLENBURG

CHARLOTTE

Tallest Building in the Carolinas

N.C.N.B. Plaza, a glass tower at the corner of Tryon and Trade Streets, is the tallest building between Philadelphia and Atlanta.

Completed in 1974, the building is 503.5 feet tall and has 40 stories. It has 880,000 square feet of floor space, 754,291 of which are usable as office space, making it one of the largest office buildings in the Southeast. The building is headquarters for N.C.N.B. Corporation and Bank. It has no observation deck, and a 40th floor dining room is not open to the public.

Wing Haven

When Elizabeth Clarkson married her husband Edwin and came to Charlotte in 1927 to see for the first time the house he had built for her, she found it sitting on an outlying red clay lot with a single spindly willow oak to shelter it.

This would not do, she said. So they bought some adjoining lots and set about building a garden. For years, on anniversaries, birthdays and other special occasions, they gave each other 1,000 bricks. They used those bricks to build a walled 3 1/2-acre garden with stream, pools, walkways, trees, shrubs and flowers that became not only a sanctuary for birds but also a place of respite for anybody seeking peace, quiet and a touch of nature in the center of teeming Charlotte.

Birds flock to the garden with its many feeders, and 130 species have been spotted there, including green herons, kingfishers and wood ducks. Many of the birds are so tame that they feed from Elizabeth's hand.

In 1975, the Clarksons gave their garden to a foundation to be kept in perpetuity. It is at 248 Ridgewood Avenue in southeast Charlotte's Myers Park area and is open Monday–Wednesday, 3–5, at no charge. Pictures of birds likely to be seen in different seasons are posted and trees, shrubs and plants are identified by markers. For information call Ann McElwee at (704) 375-5873.

World's Ugliest Statue
Of Martin Luther King Jr.

In the late '70s, a drive was started in Charlotte to raise $68,000 to erect a statue of slain civil rights leader Martin Luther King Jr. When the money was raised, Selma Burke, a black sculptor born in North Carolina, living in New Hope, Pennsylvania, was commissioned to do the bronze statue.

When the statue was unveiled in April, 1980, it stirred quite a controversy. The problem was, said critics, that it didn't look like King. The face was too lean. The nose, chin and forehead weren't right. It was ugly, they said. Just didn't look like him.

The sculptor replied that she had tried to capture the spirit of King more than the likeness.

"I put down what I felt more than what I saw," she was quoted as saying.

That didn't mollify the critics who said they wished she'd felt like making it look enough like King to make him recognizable. Some even suggested sawing the head off and replacing it.

But nothing came of it, and the statue still stands in Marshall Park on East Third Street downtown.

SHUFFLETOWN

Mayday-Mayday Festival

This is how Shuffletown, a crossroads community on N.C. Highway 16, eight miles northwest of Charlotte, got its name: In the 1800s. farmers from a wide area would gather at a country store at the crossroads, and a fellow by the name of Sam Oglesby would dispense spirits for a nickel a dipperful.

When an angry wife confronted her husband and demanded to know what he'd been doing at the store, he responded by saying, "Nothin', just shufflin' around."

1929 — 1968
DR. MARTIN LUTHER KING. JR.
"WHO DARED TO MAKE THE AMERICAN
DREAM OF FREEDOM FOR ALL
AMERICANS A REALITY"

World's ugliest statue of Martin Luther King, Jr.

"After a dipper of that stuff, shufflin's about all you can do," she said with a snort.

In 1983, some Shuffletown residents decided it was time to cele- brate their heritage and organized the first Shuffletown Mayday- Mayday Festival.

Events included yard and bake sales and a parade that stood still while spectators walked around it, providing their own band music with transistor radios. Visitors were able to buy small jars of Shuffletown dirt, deeds to an inch of Shuffletown property, "Onery Shuffletown Citizen" certificates and Shuffletown t-shirts, as well as enjoy the specialty at the Shuffletown Grill, baloney burgers.

Plans call for adding an outdoor drama about Shuffletown's history to future festivals on the first weekend in May—if some Shuffletown citizen can find the energy to write one.

"We stumbled across some funny history," says Judy Coffin, one of the organizers.

MONTGOMERY

BLACK ANKLE

Black Ankle Fort

Black Ankle, a community near the Randolph County line, once had quite a reputation as a rough and rowdy bootleg liquor center. In fact, that's how the community got its name. Bootleggers would build many fires to distract law officers from the fires of their stills, and it was said that they got black ankles from walking through all the ashes.

The community was so rough that Lester Singleton, who admits to making a little liquor himself once upon a time, used to joke that Black Ankle ought to have a fort.

So he built one.

It started as a simple stone house for his family on his 12 rocky acres. It grew into a fantasy land, built mostly from junk that Lester, a trash hauler, salvaged from dumps and other places. To the front of his house, Lester added a big public room with stone furnishings, an indoor pool filled with bream and catfish. This he made into a recreation room and display area for the old things and oddities he has collected.

Outside, he built covered walkways, gardens, a waterfall, a mystery house where gravity is defied, a fun house filled with gags and his extensive bottle collection, a spook house and carnival—like game booths. All of it he enclosed in a stockade of bamboo and birch. Out by the road he put a sign that says, "Black Ankle Fort."

The fort became not only a community gathering place but a popular spot for visitors, strangers who heard about it. Lester loves to show visitors around at no cost.

"We're going to be doin' something as long as we live, you know it?" he says. "And I'd just as soon be doin' something like this as anything. I love to fool around here."

Lester's fort is on State Road 1354. Turn at Asbury Church, just off U.S. Highway 220, about one mile south of the Randolph County line.

Lester Singleton and Black Ankle Fort

Black Ankle Fort: Lester's water wheel

Black Ankle Fort: Lester in part of garden

MOORE

PARKWOOD

Millstone Ghost Town

Nobody knows what happened to Parkewood or its residents. What is known is that the town was founded in 1880 after Lewis Grimm discovered a large deposit of conglomerite, a blue granite impregnated with chips of hard white quartz that was used for making millstones. He founded a company on the site of the deposit and began making portable grist mills. The town of Parkewood grew around the company, and it came to have several hundred residents, a company store and a two-story hotel.

Then early in the 1890s something happened. The company closed and the town was suddenly abandoned.

"No one knows why they left or where they went to," says Moore County historian Thurman Maness. "The workers just rode off and left their houses and everything behind."

Up until the 1920s, the town remained intact and drew lots of curiosity seekers. But vandals and nature took their course, and all the buildings eventually collapsed. The stone remains are now overgrown with trees. The town site, which isn't marked, is in a valley about 50 yards off N.C. Highway 22, just south of the community of Parkwood, which took its name from the old town.

PINEHURST

America's Largest Croquet Center

Pinehurst, known worldwide for its golf courses, may soon be equally well known for its croquet courts.

In 1982, the Pinehurst Hotel and Country Club installed four regulation lawn courts for croquet—an ancient game played with mallets, balls and wickets and favored by the rich—and hired a croquet professional, Peyton Ballenger, one of only two such persons in America.

"I think it's going to be one of the great centers of croquet in the nation," Jack Osborn, president of the U.S. Croquet Association, said of the facility.

No other club in America has as many croquet courts on the same site. Professional tournaments are being planned for the courts, which can be rented by the hour. For information call (919) 295-6811. Other sanctioned croquet clubs in North Carolina are at nearby Southern Pines, Salisbury, Linville and Aulander.

World Golf Hall of Fame

Want to see the world's finest collection of golf tees, pencils, balls and clubs? How about Dwight Eisenhower's personal golf cart?

Want to know the year-by-year hole-in-one records for golfers, amateur and professional? Want to know the story of golf from its crude beginnings in Scotland?

If so, the World Golf Hall of Fame is for you.

Pinehurst, which sports five world-class golf courses, with more than a dozen other courses within a few minutes drive, became one of America's first and finest golfing centers, so when it was decided that golf should have a hall of fame to honor its best players, like baseball's in Cooperstown, New York, Pinehurst was a prime spot for it.

The World Golf Hall of Fame opened in a $2.5 million shrine in 1974, and all of golf's big names showed up for the dedication by President Gerald Ford. The Hall of Fame has seen some troubled financial times since, but continues to operate as a non-profit organization.

On Gerald Ford Boulevard off Midland Road, the shrine and museum are open 9–5 daily. Admission is charged for persons over 16.

SOUTHERN PINES

Writer's Haven

James Boyd, born in Pennsylvania, returned from World War I to settle in a house his grandfather built in Southern Pines. A Princeton graduate who'd studied at Trinity College in Cambridge before the war, Boyd had been encouraged to write by English novelist John Galsworthy.

He published several short stories in the early '20s, and in 1925 his first and most famous novel, *Drums,* set in the Revolutionary War, appeared to great acclaim.

Before his death in 1944, Boyd published five more novels, bought the local newspaper, *The Pilot,* and transformed his grandfather's house into a Georgian mansion of some 30 rooms. While Boyd and his wife Katherine lived in the house, which they called Weymouth, they made it a haven for writers. Galsworthy visited there, as did F. Scott Fitzgerald, Thomas Wolfe and editor Maxwell Perkins. Sherwood Anderson wrote short stories at the house and North Carolina playwright Paul Green worked there on a play.

At her death in 1974, Katherine Boyd left her home to Sandhills Community College. In 1979 the college sold it to a group called Friends of Weymouth for $700,000, to be turned into a center for arts and humanities. Scores of North Carolina writers have since come to the house for short periods as writers in residence.

Exhibits and special events are frequently held at the center, which is open to visitors Monday–Friday, 10 a.m.–noon and 2–4 p.m. Weymouth is on Vermont Avenue.

America's Largest Stand of Virgin Pines

Weymouth Estate, owned by novelist James Boyd, includes about 150 acres of virgin longleaf pines, some believed to be as much as 400 years old, the largest such stand in the nation. State foresters have compared the trees in significance to California's redwoods.

The pines are now overseen by the state parks division as part of the adjoining Weymouth Woods Nature Preserve, some 400 acres given to the state in 1963 by Boyd's widow, Katherine. The preserve, on Ft. Bragg Road, off U.S. Highway 1, offers a nature museum and hiking trails and is open daily at no charge.

ORANGE

CHAPEL HILL

America's Largest Post Oak

The biggest post oak tree in America is on the campus of the University of North Carolina, northwest of Old West dormitory. It's 94 feet tall with a crown spread of 92 feet. The trunk has a circumference of nearly 13 feet.

America's Oldest State University

The University of North Carolina, the first state-supported university in the new nation, opened January 15, 1795, on a wooded hill named for a small chapel called New Hope. The first student, Hinton James of

Wilmington, arrived February 12, and within two weeks, 40 more students were enrolled. They were taught by a faculty of two and lived in Old East Dorm, the cornerstone for which was laid in 1793. The building still stands and is now a national historic landmark.

Old East, America's oldest state university dorm

Largest Natural Botanical Garden in Southeast

The N.C. Botanical Garden offers 330 acres of plants native to the state, making it the largest natural botanical garden in the Southeast. Walking tours, classes and a reference library are available to visitors. Plants are sold. The garden, off the U.S. Highway 15-501 Bypass, is open Monday-Friday, 8 a.m.-5 p.m.; Saturday, 10 a.m.-4 p.m.; and Sunday, 2-5 p.m.

World's First University Planetarium

John Motley Morehead, chemist, industrialist and leading benefactor of the University of North Carolina, became intrigued with a planetarium he visited while a diplomat in Sweden in the '40s. He liked it so much that he bought it in 1948 and shipped it as a gift to the University of North

Carolina at Chapel Hill, making it the first university-owned planetarium in the world.

Since its opening in 1949, millions of visitors have come to the 500-seat planetarium on Franklin Street on the campus. Built in Germany in 1930, the planetarium is one of the world's largest, capable of simulating the appearance of the sky from any point on or near earth for 26,000 years in the past or future on its 68-foot dome. From 1960 to 1975 all of America's astronauts came to the planetarium to learn celestial navigation.

Morehead Planetarium, which also offers art and science exhibits, has shows nightly at 8, plus Saturday shows at 11, 1, 3, and Sunday shows at 2 and 3 p.m. Admission is charged.

HILLSBOROUGH

Hog Day

No hogs inhabit Hillsborough. They are forbidden by law. There aren't even many hogs in the surrounding countryside. Hogs rank behind tobacco, eggs, poultry and beef cattle in the county's lineup of agricultural production. But in 1983, the town proclaimed an annual Hog Day celebration. Why?

Well, some folks in town decided they ought to have a festival but didn't know what kind. So they held a contest in the county schools and let students suggest what to celebrate. A high school sophomore, a hog farmer's daughter, suggested Hog Day and won.

The celebration is held the third weekend in June in the center of town. At the first one, visitors could go hog wild petting baby pigs, eating barbecued ones, or buying hog hats and t-shirts, inflatable pigs, hogs-and-kisses coffee mugs and chances on a large stuffed toy hog.

Highlight of the event is the hog calling contest. Participants in the first one used calls ranging from the traditional "Sue-e-e-e-e" to a high-pitched, hair-raising "He-e-e-e-e-a-a-ah, pig, he-e-e-e-e-a-a-ah, pig."

The winner, Fred McPherson, a Hillsborough grain salesman who grew up on a hog farm in Columbus County, used a "Who-o-o-o-o, piggy, who-o-o-o-o, piggy, who-o-o-o."

Music Box Museum

Doyle Lane, a Michigan native, was a Xerox salesman when he bought an old player piano and fixed it. He enjoyed it so much that he bought another one.

"One thing led to another," he says.

Next thing he knew he'd given up his job and was buying, repairing, selling and collecting music-making devices of all sorts, ranging from huge Orchestrions—an orchestra in a box—to tiny, delicate snuff music boxes. He opened his first music box museum in Vancouver, Canada, where he was living at the time, but moved it to Hillsborough in 1978.

The museum features more than 100 mechanical music makers of all sizes, some dating back more than 130 years, all functioning. Several are one-of-a-kind pieces, including what is believed to be the only remaining Resatone Grand, a player grisicot, which makes music with the sound of marimba bells. Doyle believes his collection to be one of the world' finest.

The museum, which also includes antique toys, steam whistles, sheet music and other items, is in Daniel Boone Village at exit 164 on Interstate Highway 85. It's open Monday–Saturday, 8:30–6; Sunday, 12–6; for a fee.

RANDOLPH

ASHEBORO

Oldest Mountains in North America

Some geologists believe the Uwharrie Mountains of Randolph, Stanly, Davidson and Montgomery counties to be the oldest in North America and among the oldest in the world.

These mountains may date back 600 million years and are believed to have once towered 20,000 feet. Worn by time, most of the peaks are now only 800 to 1,000 feet.

Within the range are Morrow Mountain State Park, the Uwharrie National Forest, four lakes along the Yadkin River—High Rock, Tuckertown, Badin and Tillery—and the N.C. Zoological Park and Gardens, which when completed near century's end will be the largest natural habitat zoo in the world.

A 33-mile hiking trail, developed by Boy Scouts, is maintained in the range. The northern terminus is on State Road 1142, six miles southwest of Asheboro, the southern terminus on N.C. Highway 24–27, six miles east of Albemarle. A detailed guide and map of the trail by Nicholas Hancock can be bought in area stores.

LEVEL CROSS

Richard Petty Fan Club Convention

Richard Petty is the most famous and successful stock-car racer of all time. At the end of the 1983 season, he had won 198 races and more than five million dollars, a record unlikely to be equalled.

Richard followed his father, Lee, into racing, and his own son, Kyle, is now a racer.

The family built a large racing complex in Level Cross, next door to Lee's house, and here each summer in June or July, the Richard Petty Fan Club gathers for its annual convention. Activities include tours of the garage and huge trophy room, watching racing events, participating in pit crew races, and of course, posing for snapshots with Richard. Usually, more than 1,000 people attend. Fan club membership, available from Lynn Myers, 117 Brentwood Drive, Willow Grove, Pennsylvania, is required for admission.

Four times in the past, Richard has held open house at Petty Enterprises. At the most recent one, in 1983, more than 50,000 people showed up, creating a massive traffic jam in Level Cross. Thousands waited hours in line to meet Richard and get his autograph. Open houses are not regularly scheduled.

Petty Enterprises is on Petty Road, off U.S. Highway 220 business.

SEAGROVE

America's Pottery Center

Underlying the rolling hills of Randolph and Moore Counties is a blue-veined clay that makes good pottery. It was discovered in the 1730s, and by the 1740s a community of potters had begun to grow in the area. It became a principal pottery center in the early days of the nation's history. And some of the same families making pottery in the area then—Cravens, Coles, Owens, Teagues—are still making it today.

Revived in this century, the area's pottery—particularly that made by the late Ben Owen at Jugtown—became world famous, shown in many of the world's largest museums, including a permanent display at the Smithsonian Institution.

Examples of the area's pottery from its earliest days to the present can be seen at the Seagrove Potters Museum on U.S. Highway 220 on the north side of Seagrove. Opened in 1980 in the old Seagrove depot, the museum features more than 2,000 pieces of area pottery in the collection of Walter and Dorothy Auman (Dorothy was a Cole), who moved the dilapidated depot from its original site to a spot next to their pottery. The museum features pictures of old area potters as well as examples of their work. Maps to the workshops of some 20 area potters are available at the museum, which is open without charge Monday--Saturday, 10-4.

In 1982, a pottery festival was started in Seagrove. Area potters display and sell their wares as well as give demonstrations. The festival is held the third Sunday of November at Seagrove School (behind the lumber plant, just off U.S. Highway 220). A limited edition auction is also held. Admission is charged. Plans call for using profits from the festival to build a second, larger pottery museum in Seagrove.

RICHMOND

HAMLET

America's Longest
Straight Stretch of Railroad Tracks

The Seaboard System railroad tracks that begin in Hamlet and run southeast to Wilmington have no turns for 78.8 miles and are the longest straight stretch of railroad tracks in America. Only a 300-mile straight stretch of the Trans-Australian Railway is longer.

National Railroad Museum and Hall of Fame

Hamlet has been a railroad town for more than 100 years. It's a hub from which the Seaboard System sends freight cars in many directions. At one time, when passenger trains were still common, 42 a day stopped at Hamlet's picturesque railroad station, the only railroad station in the state honored with a state highway historic marker. Now only one passenger train, the New York-to-Florida Silver Star stops, once a day heading south, once north. But if you want to board in Hamlet, you have to get your ticket somewhere else, because the ticket window closed in 1983.

A group of retired railroadmen are determined to keep the town's railroad station alive, though, and they've opened the National Railroad Museum and Hall of Fame, a big name for a small museum, in two rooms of the station. There they display memorabilia ranging from old conductors' uniforms to dating nails used to tell the railroad when track ties were put down. A replica of the Raleigh, the first steam engine in the state, may be seen, along with a photo of the Seaboard Limited, the first New York-to-Florida train. One room is a reproduction of an old telegrapher's office.

The free museum, in the center of town, is open Saturday and Sunday, 2-5, but old railroadmen can be found at the station telling stories almost any day. Group showings can be arranged at other times by calling Dan Bennett at (919) 582-4387.

ROCKINGHAM

MADISON

The Hubcap King Museum

"Don't you think they're pretty hanging up?" Bob Smith, the Hubcap King, said. "I like to look at 'em. I look at 'em every day, rearrange 'em. I work with 'em constantly. I just like to fool with hubcaps to tell you the truth. Yessir, I'm completely fascinated with 'em."

Bob Smith was a car dealer in Madison for 30 years. After his dealership closed, leaving him with a big empty building, he opened an antiques shop in it. He discovered a few old hubcaps in the garage and hung them on the wall for decoration.

"That was a blank wall, see," he explained, "and I thought it would look better with a hubcap on it. I put some up there and it looked so good I went out and got some more and put 'em up there. Started up the front yonder with about 20 hubcaps. Then I began to fill it up."

The collection grew to about 3,000, each lovingly attended by Bob Smith.

"I wash 'em just like it was a baby, inside and out. I just think they're all pretty. I tell you, if I had it to do over, I wouldn't fool with nothin' but hubcaps. I love antiques, but I love my hubcaps better."

The museum is at 107 Franklin Street. For information call (919) 548-2225.

REIDSVILLE

America's Second-Largest Horseshoeing Contest

Farriers from more than 20 states pound and rasp in the annual competition of the North Carolina–Virginia Horseshoeing Association on the second weekend in November. Started in 1976, the contest is second in size only to the national championships, which are held in a different place every year.

Senior, intermediate and novice farriers compete in making different types of shoes, as well as in shoeing different types of horses and mules. The event is held at Flat Rock Farm on N.C. Highway 158, about eight miles west of Reidsville.

North Carolina Wild Foods Weekend

Just what is poke salad anyway? Find out at the North Carolina Wild Foods Weekend, where you also can sample peppergrass, clover blossoms, dandelion greens, daisies, cattails, thistles, dock, burdock and many other plants commonly called weeds.

Edeline Wood, a wild foods expert and protege of the late Euell Gibbons, leads seminars and foraging expeditions to identify, gather and prepare wild foods. A grand wild foods feast is the highlight of the weekend.

The event is held at the Betsy-Jeff Penn 4-H Center near Reidsville. Participation is limited on a first-come, first-served basis for a fee. Participants may choose from two plans, one providing seminars and meals, the other including lodging in rustic dormitory cottages. For information write N.C. Wild Foods Weekend, P.O. Box 396, Elon College, N.C. 27244.

ROWAN

CLEVELAND

Grave of Napoleon's General?

The marker on the brick mausoleum is simple: "In memory of Peter

Stewart Ney, a native of France and soldier of the French Revolution under Napoleon Bonaparte who departed this life Nov. 15th, 1846, aged 77 years."

Was Peter Ney in fact Napoleon's famed general Marshal Michael Ney—called "Red Peter" by some—who supposedly was executed by a firing squad in Paris after the Battle of Waterloo? Many people came to believe so.

Peter Ney was a school teacher who drifted into central North Carolina and moved frequently. He worshiped Napoleon and had astonishing knowledge of the Napoleonic wars. In books about the French Revolution that he borrowed from libraries, he frequently penciled in corrections. He possessed all the physical attributes of Marshal Ney, even battle scars, and was, like Marshal Ney, an expert swordsman. Once while riding in a parade in Columbia, S.C., he was recognized as Marshal Ney by a Frenchman then living in Charleston.

In his classroom when word came of Napoleon's death, Peter Ney fainted and that night attempted suicide.

While Ney made no public claims to being the marshal, he reportedly confided to friends that he was and even told them the story of how he escaped the firing squad and made his way to this country. Questioned on his death bed, he acknowledged that he was indeed the famous general.

"The old guard is defeated," he is quoted as saying. "Now let me die."

Ney is buried in the cemetery of Third Creek Presbyterian Church in the community of Cleveland, off U.S. Highway 70, in northwestern Rowan County, where he taught.

SALISBURY

Luther Sowers's Medieval Armory
And Chastity Belt Forge

Luther Sowers doesn't know what brought it on; he just knows that the interest was there even when he was growing up on a farm near Salisbury.

"I can remember taking tin off the chicken house and making Roman armor," he recalls.

In high school, he made armor for Latin Club presentations, and even after he went away to study sculpture for five years at the Tyler School of Art at Temple University in Philadelphia, his fascination continued. After he returned to North Carolina to teach art in public schools in Wilson, his interest in ancient military paraphernalia grew even greater. He began making swords, dirks and other weapons, uniforms and insignia.

In 1974, he quit teaching and returned to his family farm where he built a small studio and foundry and began making military reproductions. Items of armor and chain mail, a sort of metal fabric impenetrable by swords, are a specialty.

A few years ago, Luther gained national attention when he saw a letter in the Dear Abby column from a woman who had a very jealous husband and thought his anxieties might be relieved if she wore a chastity belt. Her problem was that she couldn't find one.

Luther wrote Abby offering to make an authentic chastity belt for the woman, and the letter appeared in her column. The results: lots of orders for military equipment but none for chastity belts. Just in case, Luther had done a thorough study of chastity belts and was prepared to make them, although he said he would try to talk any prospective buyers out of the idea.

"The things were extremely uncomfortable and very unsanitary, horribly unsanitary, very difficult to clean," he said. "Anybody coming back from a long trip and unlocking the merchandise would probably not want to have anything to do with it."

Luther's studio and exhibits of armor and weaponry are four miles west of Salisbury on U.S. Highway 70 and may be seen by appointment. Call (704) 633-4170.

SPENCER

America's Largest Transportation Museum

At the turn of the century, Southern Railway built the largest steam locomotive repair shop in the South at Spencer. It included a 37-stall roundhouse and a repair shop the size of four football fields. In 1983, the North Carolina Transportation Museum opened in the old facility. Called Spencer Shops, it is the largest such museum in the country and the largest of any type in North Carolina.

Visitors can see a slide-show history of the shops in a yellow refrigerated car before entering the warehouse museum where they can examine exhibits ranging from Indian canoes to airplanes.

A handmade Conestoga wagon, old fire-fighting equipment, and many old cars and trucks are displayed. Railroad cars exhibited include Doris, the private car of North Carolina-born tycoon James Buchanan Duke.

Other exhibits range from a huge collection of highway signs to functioning diesel and gasoline engines and old railroad lanterns. The museum, on Salisbury Avenue (U.S. Highway 29-70), is open Monday-Saturday, 9-5; Sunday 1-5; at no charge.

STANLY

NEW LONDON

The Only Functioning Gold Mine
In the Southeast

Glenn Nance grew up near Denton in Davidson County plowing rocky fields, working in sawmills and dreaming of gold.

"I've thought about gold purty much since I was a little boy," he says. "I would read these gold stories, how some got rich, some got killed, some went broke. I'd take a pie pan and slip off down to the branch and try to find some gold. I had it in my mind that I'd cut off one day and find some."

It took a while but Glenn eventually did just that. He was in the grading business when a fellow said he'd like Glenn to help him determine if there was any gold on his old homeplace.

Glenn made one cut along a hillside on the fellow's land and turned up gold aplenty.

"I took out five pockets of gold," he remembers, "and one of 'em carried thirteen hundred and sixty-seven quartz rock with gold and over one pound of pure nugget gold, some of 'em weighing over an ounce apiece."

Two years later, Glenn bought 22 acres of the land and within a few years he'd given up his grading business, moved into a trailer on the land and taken up mining. He has since dug three deep shafts, doing all the work himself, hauling out the ore in 15-gallon buckets.

He allows amateur panners to work the ore for a small fee and keep all the gold they find. Some have panned out large amounts.

The Cotton Patch Mine, so named because cotton once grew on the land, also supplies the ore that is panned at Reed Gold Mine in Cabarrus County, the first gold mine in America, the mine that set off America's first gold rush. To get to Cotton Patch go east on East Gold Street and follow the signs. The mine is open from March 1 to October 31.

STOKES

DILLARD

Roger Dodger Convention

Pompey Cardwell was a lifeguard teaching children to swim when he decided his class should have a name. He called them Roger Dodgers. The children had so much fun with the secret handshake and chant Pompey devised that he made the Roger Dodgers into an informal club and inducted any child who would pay a penny for lifetime membership, vow to be a faithful Roger Dodger and give Pompey a snapshot of him- or herself to put on the wall of his room in a Madison Tobacco warehouse.

Pompey's room became covered with snapshots of Roger Dodgers, and as some of them grew up and moved away, they held to their Roger Dodger vows, kept in touch with their exalted leader, Mac Pete, as Pompey is called, and spread the Roger Dodger Club throughout the

world. Many brought their own children to be sworn in as Roger
Dodgers.

Each year on the third weekend in July Roger Dodgers hold an
annual convention, an all-day party to pay homage to their exalted
leader, who in recent years has been confined to a wheelchair by a
stroke.

The convention is held at Roger Dodger Land, a six-acre tract
bearing the official Roger Dodger Headquarters, a log cabin built by
Pompey himself, just off N.C. Highway 772, off U.S. Highway 311, about
ten miles west of Madison.

SURRY

MT. AIRY

Grave of Original Siamese Twins

Although there were recorded births of joined twins before the 19th
century, the first such twins to gain worldwide attention were born in
the Southeast Asian land of Siam, now Thailand, thus giving the des-
cription Siamese twins to all such children.

The twin boys, joined at the chest by a band of cartilage and flesh,
were born of Chinese peasant parents in May, 1811. Their mother
named them Chang and Eng and required them as youngsters to
strenuously exercise their connecting band until they were able to stand
side by side and live as normally as possible.

At 14, while working as peddlers in Bangkok, the twins met and
befriended a Scottish trader, Robert Hunter. Four years later, Hunter
teamed with an American ship captain, Abel Coffin, to bring the boys to
the United States in the hope of exhibiting them for profit.

The boys arrived in Boston in August, 1829, and were an immediate sensation. They went on to New York, then to London, drawing
huge crowds. As their fame spread, they went to work for flamboyant

showman Phineas Barnum and became his second-most popular attraction after Tom Thumb.

By the time they were in their mid-20s, the twins were touring the country on their own. They had won American citizenship and taken the family name Bunker, offered them by a New York man named Fred Bunker in a chance encounter at the naturalization office. In June, 1837, they scheduled a show in the North Carolina town of Wilkesboro in the green foothills of the Blue Ridge Mountains.

Tired of traveling and exhibiting themselves, the twins became entranced by Wilkesboro's countryside and decided to stay. They opened a store which failed, and two years later, they bought 110 acres in the Trap Hill community, built a home and became farmers and wood cutters.

The twins had longed for marriage and families but that seemed impossible before they met Sarah and Adelaide Yates, daughters of a neighboring farmer. A scandal ensued when the twins appeared in public with the sisters, and the four were ordered not to see each other again. They continued to meet secretly, however, and Chang and Eng, desperate to be married, went to the College of Surgery in Philadelphia and requested an operation to separate them.

The twins had already been examined by some of the world's leading medical experts, who had decided that separation was too risky. Doctors at Philadelphia didn't want to attempt the operation, but the twins insisted. Meanwhile, Sarah and Adelaide learned of their plans, rushed to Philadelphia, begged them not to go through with it and promised to marry them as they were.

The four returned to Wilkes County and on April 13, 1843, in their local Baptist church, Chang was married to Adelaide, then 19, and Eng to Sarah, then 20. The twins were just a month shy of their 32nd birthday.

The four moved into the twins' house and both twins soon fathered children. With their families burgeoning and quarelling, the twins bought land in the White Plains section of adjoining Surry County, near Mount Airy, and built each twin a house a mile apart. Afterwards, the twins spent three days in one house, then three at the other, never varying their pattern. Chang eventually fathered 10 children, Eng 12.

The twins got along remarkably well considering that they had different personalities and interests. Chang drank; Eng was a teetotaler. Eng liked to sit up playing poker with friends; Chang would nod off. Chang was irritable; Eng even-tempered. A keen sense of humor in both helped them accept their predicament.

Once when they got into a fight atop a hay wagon, Chang held Eng down.

"If you don't let go, so help me, I'll throw you off this wagon," Eng threatened. Then both broke into laughter, realizing the absurdity of the statement.

The two families thrived until the Civil War when hard times came. After the war, Chang and Eng, then well into their 50s, were again drawn into show business to try to make money. While touring Europe, they consulted the top medical authorities in England, Germany and France about separation, but it was again ruled out.

On the way home, Chang suffered a stroke, leaving him partially paralyzed and deaf. Afterward, he began drinking heavily and his health deteriorated even more, alarming Eng, whose health remained good. To no avail, Eng pleaded for Chang to stop drinking.

In January, 1874, Chang developed severe bronchitis and chest pains and was told by his doctor to stay in bed, but when time came for him to move to Eng's home for three days, he insisted on going. At Eng's home, Chang was unable to sleep, suffered chills and wanted to sit up at night, much to Eng's discomfort. In the early morning hours of January 17, Eng insisted that they go to bed. Chang agreed, and a few hours later, Eng awoke to discover Chang's labored breathing had ceased. He called for help, and family members rushed to his side. A son told Eng that Chang was dead.

"Then I am going, too," Eng said and became hysterical, sweating and twisting, as if trying to shake free of his dead brother. While some family members tried to calm him, others rushed to fetch the doctor three miles away in Mt. Airy and to tell Chang's family of his death. Within an hour, Eng had slipped into a coma. After another hour, he died before the doctor arrived.

Two weeks after the twins' deaths, their families allowed a limited autopsy. It showed that a small artery passed through their connecting band, which would have made separating them difficult at the time. It also showed that Eng was obviously healthy and apparently died from fright.

The families wouldn't allow the twins to be separated in death, and they were buried in a large tin coffin in the Baptist church cemetery. Eng's wife, Sarah, who died in 1892, and Chang's wife, Adelaide, who died at age 94 in 1917, later joined them in the plot. The grave is at Old White Plains Baptist Church on old U.S. Highway 601, two miles west of Mt. Airy.

UNION

MONROE

America's Largest Rabbit Club Shows

The Union Rabbit Breeders Club is the largest and fastest growing in the United States, with more than 200 members in North Carolina and South Carolina. Twice a year, it holds shows where hundreds of rabbits of most known breeds are displayed, including some of the finest of their breed.

Breeds include New Zealand White, Californian, Netherland Dwarf, Dutch, Rex, Belgian Hare, Flemish Giant, Satin and Chinchilla, among many others.

"There's a shape and size of rabbit for everybody in the world," says club president Les Everett.

Club shows are open to the public at no charge. They are held the second Saturday in March and the last Saturday in September at Dickerson Center off Johnson Street. For information, call Les at (704) 283-5430.

WAXHAW

Old Hickory Festival

For nearly 200 years, North Carolinians and South Carolinians have argued over the birthplace of Andrew Jackson, "Old Hickory," as he was called, hero of the Battle of New Orleans, seventh president of the United States.

North Carolinians claim he was born near Waxhaw, just north of the South Carolina line. South Carolinians say it was at McCamie Park, just south of the North Carolina line.

To settle the issue, at least temporarily, residents of Union County, N.C., and Lancaster County, S.C., got together and staged an annual football game, played by the best players from each county's four high schools. The winning team claims bragging rights to Old Hickory's birthplace for the coming year.

In conjunction with the football game, which is always played in Lancaster, Waxhaw stages a four-day Old Hickory Festival with arts and crafts, street dancing, music, a parade and other events.

Since 1979, when the festival began, it has been held the last weekend in August. That may change in 1984 to the last weekend in September. For information, call Dottie Shaw at (704) 843-3141.

WAKE

CARY

America's Oldest Gourd Festival

North Carolina, particularly its piedmont, is purported to be one of the world's finest areas for growing hard-shell gourds. Such gourds, grown in scores of varieties, have both decorative and practical uses, and almost every conceivable use for them can be seen at Cary's annual Gourd Festival on the third weekend of September.

Cary calls itself America's Gourd Capital. The first gourd club in America was formed in the town in 1939, and two years later it started the country's first gourd festival.

The event draws hundreds of gourd fanciers from many areas to display gourds and exchange gourds, seeds and ideas. It's held at Jordan Hall on North Harrison Avenue. For information call (919) 469-4000.

FUQUAY-VARINA

World's Only Gourd Museum

Marvin Johnson was a math teacher and high school coach for 20 years before he quit to return to his homeplace, care for his aging parents and take up tobacco farming. One day he discovered in the attic some old gourds his mother had hung to dry years earlier and decided to plant some of the seeds.

"It just grew from that," he said.

What grew was one of the world's great gourd collections—gourds from all over the world. Marvin eventually grew more than 200 varieties and became one of the world's top gourd experts and leading fanciers. He has developed new gourds and rediscovered gourds thought to be extinct.

He has grown thousands of gourds every year—and given them all away.

"Lot of people ask me, 'Why don't you sell the gourds?'" he says. "Doggone, I'm not interested. I enjoy givin' people the gourds and wouldn't enjoy sellin' 'em."

Marvin sent gourds all over the world to acquaintances he made through the American Gourd Society. And inevitably gourds came back. Painted gourds, carved gourds, gourds hundreds of years old. Gourds made into toys, pipes, hats, dolls, animals, musical instruments.

By 1965, Marvin's house was so filled with gourds that he built a building for them in woods near his house and opened the world's only gourd museum. He put this sign on the wall: "There's an old legend that says if you give or receive a gourd . . . with it goes all the beauty of life in health, happiness and other good things."

Thousands of people have visited the museum since it opened, including once-famous fan dancer Sally Rand. The museum is always open at no charge. Near it is a nature trail, and Marvin has provided picnic tables and restrooms on a nearby lake for visitors. The museum is on N.C. Highway 55 south.

LIZARD LICK

Lizard Lick Lizard Races

The story is told that a fellow named Pulley, generally called Ol' Man Pulley, owned a government-sanctioned liquor (generally called likker) still in eastern Wake County in the last century. Ol' Man Pulley was the official taster as well as maker of the likker, and along about mid-afternoon he'd be a little unsteady on his feet and feel the need for a walk.

The still was surrounded by a rail fence, and Ol' Man Pulley would walk around it, keeping track by tapping the fence with his cane. Lizards favored the fence for sunning, and Ol' Man Pulley would whack at them with his cane as he went.

"There goes Ol' Man Pulley with his lizard licker," people would say.

And that, supposedly, is how Lizard Lick, a community of some 40 souls, got its name.

Lizard Lick always had trouble maintaining its identity, primarily because people kept stealing the community's highway sign. But never did it face a greater identity problem than it did in 1975 when the state opened a new U.S. Highway 64 bypass around the community. With the main highway no longer passing through the community and its road number changed to N.C. Highway 97, Lizard Lick was all but isolated from passersby.

Charles Wood, a Lizard Lick garage owner, wasn't about to let his community be bypassed and forgotten. He mounted a successful campaign to get Lizard Lick on state highway maps and started an annual Lizard Lick Festival with lizard races to attract attention to the community.

The event drew so much attention that Charles Wood was elected honorary mayor. He even opened a town hall and Chamber of Commerce in a building at his garage where he sold Lizard Lick bumper stickers, t-shirts and souvenirs.

Each year to promote the festival Charles came up with a new gimmick. One year it was a plan to build an amusement park called Three Flags Over Lizard Lick. Another year it was a mock Lizard Lick University offering honorary degrees. The festival, with Blue Grass music, square dancing and other events, grew so large that the community had trouble accommodating all the people, and it was dropped for a couple of years.

But demand for the return of the lizard races, also known as the Lizard Lick Olympics, was so great that Charles revived them in 1983.

The races (bring your own lizard) are held in September. For information call Charles at (919) 365-6648.

RALEIGH

America's First State Art Museum

From the 1920s the North Carolina Art Society campaigned for North Carolina to become first to open a state art museum. In 1947, the legislature finally appropriated $1 million to begin an art collection.

The museum finally opened in 1956 in an old State Highway Department building near the capitol. In 1967, the legislature authorized a new building for the museum, but not until ten years later was ground broken. The modern new museum, delayed by bickering and construction problems, opened in April, 1983. It provides a home for the state's 6,000-piece collection, valued at more than $50 million.

The museum, on Blue Ridge Road, off the Raleigh Beltline near the state fairgrounds, is open Monday–Saturday, 10 a.m.–5 p.m.; Sunday, 1–5 p.m. at no charge.

Home of History's Most Significant Man

Professor Edwin Paget has lost track of the number of times he's been honored as History's Most Significant Man, but he keeps a close count on how many times he's run to the top of 14,110-foot Pikes Peak in Colorado—985 times at the end of the summer of 1983.

A retired N.C. State University speech professor, Paget has been running up the mountain several times a week every summer since 1950 to draw attention to one of his many theories.

The professor believes that people die far younger than necessary and that they should get stronger, not weaker, with age. He believes that people could live to be 130 or 140 if only they would regularly get enough oxygen to their brains. The way to do that, he says, is by running uphill. That's why he spends his summers running up Pikes Peak. He intends to prove his theory.

Professor Paget, who won't give his age except to say that he was born a few years one side or the other of the turn of the century, is a fountainhead of ideas and theories. He originated the Baby Olympics—athletic competitions for children ages six months to two years—to encourage babies to get enough exercise to keep a sufficient supply of oxygen flowing to their brains.

He also is the father of many inventions, including the perfect dining room table for dieters. It begins rising as soon as a diner sits at it, quickly taking the food out of reach.

Hailed as The Great Rejuvenator by a South American group and once named "The World's Greatest Brain" by the Society For Intellectual Stimulation, the professor lives in a humble abode for one so significant at 2733 Everett Drive, where he can be found running up and down his basement stairs 340 times a day getting oxygen to his brain and keeping in shape for his summertime treks up Pikes Peak.

Watermelon Bowling

North Carolina is one of the top five watermelon-growing states, and each year in July the N.C. Watermelon Association celebrates that fact by staging the N.C. Watermelon Festival at the State Farmers Market on Hodges Street.

A Watermelon Queen is crowned and watermelon contests are held. Contestants compete for trophies in a seed-spitting contest, a free-throw basketball shooting contest using watermelons, and a watermelon bowling contest to see who can knock down the most pins with three watermelons. The farmer who brings in the biggest watermelon also wins a trophy. And everybody who attends is invited to eat his fill of watermelon at no charge.

In the past the festival has been held on the last Friday or Saturday in July, but a change was being considered for 1984. Call the State Farmers Market for information at (919) 733-7417.

THE
MOUNTAINS

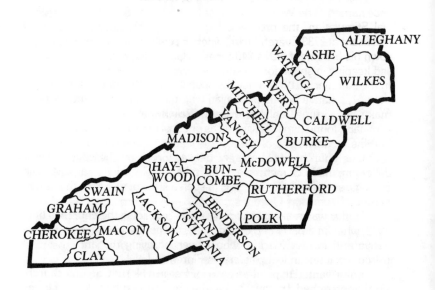

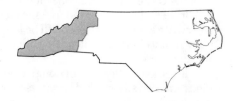

ASHE

WEST JEFFERSON

World's Only Fresco
Of Pregnant Virgin Mary

In the summer of 1972, a new Episcopal priest, Justin Faulton Hodge, then 41, a native North Carolinian who moved away to New York to make his fortune, only to discover religion at age 36 and enter a seminary, found himself assigned as priest of two tiny mission churches in Ashe County.

One church, St. Mary's, at Beaver Creek on the edge of West Jefferson, had 13 members. The other, Holy Trinity, at Glendale Springs, south of Jefferson, was in such a state of disrepair that it had closed.

Hodge was making slow progress in rebuilding the churches until 1973, when at a party in Blowing Rock, he met Ben Long, a Statesville native and former Marine, who'd been studying the ancient art of fresco—painting in wet plaster—in Florence, Italy.

Long wanted to paint a fresco for free in a North Carolina church. He'd approached 16 churches and all had turned him down. Hodge accepted immediately, and the following year Long did the first fresco, "Mary Great With Child," at St. Mary's. After it was finished, while he was working on two more frescoes at the church, "John the Baptist," and "The Mystery of Faith," Long was awarded the prestigious Leonardo da Vinci International Art Award for his work on the fresco of Mary and others in Italy, and little St. Mary's church suddenly found itself the center of international attention.

In 1978, Long returned to Ashe County to teach a class in fresco and create a huge new fresco of The Last Supper at the newly restored Holy Trinity Church at Glendale Springs, before returning to Europe to live and work.

In the fall of 1983, one of Long's students, Jeffery Mims of Southern Pines, created still another large fresco of Jesus leaving his family. It is in the church's undercroft.

The frescoes revived the two churches, which now have more than 300 members, and bring visitors to see them from all over the world—an estimated 250,000 in 1983.

St. Mary's Church is off U.S. Highway 221 at old N.C. Highway 194 at Beaver Creek near West Jefferson. Holy Trinity is on N.C. Highway 16 at Glendale Springs. The churches are always open.

Second-Oldest River on Earth

Geologists say that only the Nile in Africa is an older river than the New, which is formed when its north and south forks, rising in Watauga County, join at the Ashe–Alleghany County line. The river—like the Nile, a rare north-flowing river—meanders back and forth across the Virginia line before flowing on into West Virginia, where it joins the Kanawha at Charleston.

Controversy arose over the New in the early '70s because of a power company's plans to dam it, but the project was stopped when the federal government designated a 26.5-mile stretch of the river in Ashe County as a National Scenic River.

Clear and swift-flowing, the river is popular with canoeists and rafters, and the state has provided five stop-off points along it for overnight trips. Several outfitters in the area rent canoes and give advice about the river.

Only Cheese Plant in the Carolinas

Mountainous Ashe County has long been a dairying center. Early in this century, several small cheese-making businesses grew in the county, but in the '20s the Kraft Company bought up the small companies and consolidated them in a plant in West Jefferson, where the company made cheddar cheese from 1930 to 1975. The plant was sold in 1975 to Doug Ruddersdorf and Jerry Glick who expanded it and renamed it the Ashe County Cheese Company.

Cheddar, colby and Monterey jack cheeses are now made at the plant, and visitors are invited to watch from a glassed viewing room Monday–Saturday, 8:30–5. The company sells the cheese in an outlet across the street from the plant on Main Street.

AVERY

BANNER ELK

Woolly Worm Festival

Mountain folklore holds that the severity of a coming winter is predicted by the coat of the woolly worm, a black and brown caterpillar common in fall. If the woolly worm shows more black than brown, the winter will be bad.

Whether there is validity to that belief is frequently debated, and a long-term scientific woolly worm study undertaken by Dr. Sandra Glover at Appalachian State University in Boone has yet to reach any conclusions.

In 1977, Jim Morton, then editor of *Mountain Living Magazine*, decided he was willing to go along with the woolly worm theory, but the woolly worms he saw only confused him.

"They all looked different from each other," he says. "It was a matter of which was right and which was wrong."

It occurred to Jim that a simple way to determine which woolly worm was right about the winter would be to hold a race. The winning worm would be the official weather predictor.

Thus was born the Woolly Worm Festival. It is held each year on the third Saturday of October, and in past years it has been held on the practice football field beside the gymnasium at Lees-McRae College on N.C. Highway 184 in Banner Elk (the location may change). More than 1,000 people attend the races, and as many as 350 have paid the $5 fee to enter a favorite worm.

The worms race on three-foot strings in heats of 15 at a time. Winners then compete in crawl-offs until only one is left. The festival also includes mountain music and a gustatory treat called Woolly Worm in a blanket—a sausage dog made to resemble a woolly worm in a roll.

For more information, call Jim Morton at (704) 963-4228.

Where Marjorie Kinnan Rawlings
Wrote *The Yearling*

Marjorie Kinnan Rawlings, a former newspaper woman, came to Banner Elk seeking coolness, peace and quiet. She rented one of four cottages owned by Lees-McRae College and stayed several months working on her novel, *The Yearling*.

The story, set in Florida where Rawlings was living, was about a backwoods boy and a deer. The book became a best seller, won a Pulitzer Prize and was made into a movie starring Gregory Peck.

While in Banner Elk, Rawlings got to know a young boy from the Grandfather Home for Children next to the college who came to help her with chores. The boy inspired her most famous short story, "Mother In Manville," about an orphanage child who imagined a family.

A retired Lees-McRae English professor who met Rawlings says that she kept mostly to herself in Banner Elk.

"No one knew her well," says the woman, who asks that her name not be used. "She was just another person around writing. We had many."

The four cottages on the campus were originally built for a music camp, and two of them later were torn down. The two that remain are used as residences by college maintenance workers. No one can remember which cottage Rawlings stayed in, and no markers have been erected to note her stay. The two remaining cottages are between the college gym and the children's home.

BEECH MOUNTAIN

Highest Incorporated Town East of Rockies

Beech Mountain, a ski resort developed in the '60s, incorporated as a municipality in May, 1981, causing the summer resort town of Highlands in Macon County to have to change its welcoming signs.

For years, Highlands, elevation 4,118 feet, had proclaimed itself the highest incorporated town east of the Rockies, but that honor was claimed by Beech Mountain, elevation 5,505.

LINVILLE

The Many Amazements and Wondrous Doings
Of Grandfather Mountain

In 1885, a young mining engineer from Wilmington, Hugh MacRae, went to work for the mica mines in Mitchell County and was so taken with the surrounding mountains that he prevailed upon his father to help him buy nearly 16,000 acres of land, including Grandfather Mountain, highest peak, at 5,964 feet, in the Blue Ridge Mountains. Four years later, MacRae founded a company and began developing the first mountain golf course and Linville resort.

In 1952, following MacRae's death, his company was dissolved and his holdings divided among family members. His grandson, Hugh MacRae Morton, came into possession of 4,100-acre Grandfather Mountain (so named because from one angle the mountaintop resembles the profile of an old man looking heavenward) and began developing it as one of the state's top tourist attractions.

World's Oldest Rocks

Geologists have found that Grandfather bares some of the oldest rocks to be seen on earth, more than a billion years old, and geologists come to the mountain to study what is called the Grandfather Mountain Window, which gives them a look at what the core of earth was like when time began. The oldest of these rocks, a granite-like gneiss, can be seen along Wilson Creek, which crosses U.S. Highway 221, on the south slope of the mountain.

America's Highest Swinging Bridge

The mountaintop offers panoramic views, a visitor center with exhibits, and a natural wildlife area with bears, cougars, deer and golden and bald eagles. Perhaps the biggest attraction is the Mile High Swinging Bridge, America's highest swinging bridge, which crosses a 100-foot-deep chasm to Linville Peak. Built in 1952, the 210-foot-long bridge was designed by architect Charles Hartman Jr. to withstand the weight of three million pounds and the high winds that regularly buffet the mountaintop.

Billy Joe's Tee

Near the bridge is Billy Joe's Tee, built for N.C. amateur golfer Billy Joe Patton, who came within one shot of winning the Masters Tournament in 1954. Hugh Morton, a friend of Patton's, built the tee on the mountain's edge in honor of Billy Joe's near win so he could "knock a ball a mile." A golf ball won't sail that far off the 1,500-foot drop, but it will go a long way, and golfers who want to hit the longest ball of their lives are invited to do so. Both Ted Williams and Mickey Mantle have batted baseballs off the tee.

Eastern America's Highest Manned Weather Station

The visitor center also houses the highest manned weather station in eastern America. The mountain has some of the roughest winter weather in eastern America, and each day, regardless of conditions, Winston Church climbs the mountain to take readings. Winds of more than 100 miles per hour strike the mountain an average of 12 times a year. The highest wind recorded was 161 m.p.h. on November 18, 1976. Below zero temperatures are common in winter. The coldest was 27 below on January 11, 1982.

Masters of Hang Gliding

During summer and fall, a hang gliding team flies regularly off the peak to a landing in MacRae Meadows below. The tricky winds around the mountain make it a spot for only the most experienced pilots. Each year in August, the top 24 hang glider pilots in the world are invited to the mountain to compete in the Masters of Hang Gliding Championship, a 10-day, one-on-one racing competition.

America's Finest Highland Games and Gathering of Clans

On the second weekend in July each year, thousands of people of Scottish ancestry gather on MacRae Meadows for the Grandfather Mountain Highland Games and Gathering of the Clans, founded in 1955 by Hugh Morton's late mother, Agnes. More than 100 clans gather with tartans, kilts and bagpipes for Scottish music, dancing, flag ceremonies, sheep dog demonstrations and athletic competitions. The athletic events include caber tossing, highland wrestling and clans tug of war. *Better Homes and Gardens* has proclaimed this the finest Scottish gathering in America, and it is one of the 100 Top Events in North America.

America's Second-Toughest Marathon

A series of AAU-sanctioned track and field events is held in conjunction with the gathering, including the Mountain Marathon from Boone to Grandfather Mountain, the second-hardest marathon course in America (after the Pikes Peak Marathon in Colorado).

Singing on the Mountain

Another popular event, at times attracting as many as 50,000 people, is the annual Singing on the Mountain held in MacRae Meadows on the fourth Sunday each June. Founded by Joe Lee Hartley Sr. in 1924 as a family reunion, it was opened to all, and is the only activity on Grandfather Mountain for which no admission is charged. A day of gospel singing and preaching, the event has attracted such celebrities as Johnny Cash, Roy Acuff, Bob Hope and Oral Roberts.

Grandfather Mountain is on U.S. Highway 221 east of Linville. For more information write Grandfather Mountain, Linville, N.C. 28646, or call (704) 898-4512.

Grandfather Mountain hang glider

Grandfather Mountain: America's highest swinging bridge

Grandfather Mountain: Billy Joe Patton at his tee

Grandfather Mountain: Gathering of clans on Grandfather Mountain
Photo: Hugh Morton

World's Most Complicated Bridge

The quarter–mile Linn Cove Viaduct around the base of Grandfather Mountain, part of the missing 7.7-mile link needed to complete the 469-mile Blue Ridge Parkway, is one of the world's great engineering marvels.

The bridge, which has spiral curves going into circular curves with curvature in two directions, has seven supporting tiers 150 feet apart. It was constructed with 153 50-ton segments, none alike, only one straight. The $8-million bridge includes every kind of alignment geometry used in highway construction and is the only one of its type in America. It has attracted international attention. Begun in 1979, it was completed in 1983 but won't be put into use until the entire missing parkway segment is opened in 1987.

It can be seen from U.S. Highway 221 east of Linville.

World's most complicated bridge under construction
Photo: Hugh Morton

BUNCOMBE

ASHEVILLE

America's Largest and Finest House

George Vanderbilt was a well-educated young man who loved the finer things of life and had the money to buy them. Grandson of Commodore Cornelius Vanderbilt, builder of steamships and railroads, he had inherited a vast fortune and was using it to acquire a magnificent collection of art, books and other fine things. But where to put it all?

Why not build the biggest and finest house in America just for that purpose?

So at age 22, that's what he decided to do. He instructed a lawyer to begin buying the beautiful mountain land he had gazed upon so fondly while vacationing in Asheville, and within two years he owned 150,000 acres of it. He hired architect Richard Morris Hunt and landscape architect Frederick Law Olmstead to design and build his house for him.

It took five years to complete the 250-room mansion, and when it was finished, Christmas, 1895, it was grand indeed. Vanderbilt married soon afterward and the house became home for him, his wife, Edith, and their daughter, Cornelia. After Vanderbilt's death in 1914 at age 49, his widow gave much of the land in the estate, where the nation's first tree farm and forestry school were established, to the federal government to form the nucleus of the first national forest, Pisgah.

The estate, still in the family, now has about 11,000 acres and operates a large dairy and winery. The grounds and formal gardens, including the largest azalea garden and finest English rose garden in America, are open to the public, as are 18 rooms of the house, including the 72- by 42-foot dining hall, with its arched 75-foot ceiling, triple fireplaces and the world's largest wrought-iron chandelier, and the library with its rich walnut wood and 20,000 leather-bound rare volumes.

Several movies, including Peter Sellers's last film before his death,

Being There, have been made at the house, which is open daily, 9–5, for a fee. The estate is on U.S. Highway 25 south, near Interstate 40.

Graves of North Carolina's
Most Famous Writers

Thomas Wolfe, the flamboyant novelist, and O. Henry, master of the surprise-ending short story, both North Carolina natives, lie buried only a short distance apart in Riverside Cemetery on Birch Street, just north of Interstate Highway 240 (take Monford exit) near downtown Asheville.

Wolfe, born in 1900, died of tuberculosis of the brain at age 38. He published only two novels in his lifetime, but two more were later gleaned from his voluminous writings. His first novel, *Look Homeward Angel*, published in 1929, was autobiographical, and it shocked and infuriated many in his hometown. Asheville has since embraced and proudly acclaimed its most famous son. Wolfe's boyhood home, his mother's boarding house, Old Kentucky Home (called Dixieland in the novel), has been restored and is open to visitors for a fee. It's at 48 Spruce Street.

Wolfe is buried with his mother, father, brother and sister, and his stone bears quotations from his works.

Just down the hill from Wolfe's grave, a much smaller and simpler stone bears only the name William Sydney Porter and the dates 1862–1910.

Porter was born in Guilford County and grew up in Greensboro. As a young man, he moved to Texas, married, had a daughter, tried his hand at newspaper work and got sent to prison for misusing funds while working as a bank teller.

He began writing short stories in prison, signing them O. Henry. After his release, he moved to New York with his daughter (his wife had died) and began writing his stories for newspapers and magazines. He later renewed acquaintance with his first sweetheart in Greensboro, Sarah Coleman, who had since moved to Asheville, and they married in 1907.

Porter traveled back and forth between Asheville and New York, where he tried to write. He died in New York of alcoholism in a lonely room strewn with liquor bottles, and his wife had his body returned to Asheville for burial. She and his daughter, Margaret, are buried beside him.

F. Scott Fitzgerald's Room

F. Scott Fitzgerald, whose novels captured the Jazz Age of the '20s, was an alcoholic struggling to retain his talents when he first came to the North Carolina mountains to rest in 1935.

So taken was he with the area that in the spring of 1936, he moved his flamboyant wife, Zelda, from a Baltimore hospital, where she'd been making little progress from her mental illness, to Highland Hospital near Asheville. That summer he sold his home in Baltimore and moved into room 441 at the swank Grove Park Inn.

There he lived off and on for a year, drinking heavily (as much as 30 beers a day) and staying up late trying to write stories for magazines. Once he fired a shot in a suicide threat, prompting the hotel to require him to have a nurse.

Another time he showed up at Old Kentucky Home, the boarding

Grave of Thomas Wolfe
Photo: Greensboro News-Record

house operated by the mother of Thomas Wolfe, Asheville's own famous literary son, pretending to want to rent a room.

"I don't rent to drunks," Tom's mother, Julia, told him.

By the summer of 1937, Fitzgerald was broke and depressed. In desperation, he went to Hollywood to become a screenwriter for MGM. He died there in 1940, a broken man, age 44. Zelda died eight years later in a fire at Highland Hospital.

The room where Fitzgerald stayed is still in use, but nothing marks it as special. The hotel has had many famous guests and considers Fitzgerald as no different from the others. The hotel is on Macon Avenue, near downtown.

America's Largest Two-Wing Silverbell

The two-wing silverbell tree in George Meriwether's yard at 961 Vanderbilt Road is America's largest. It is 66.5 feet tall with a crown spread of 34 feet. The trunk is nearly six feet in circumference.

Thomas Wolfe Memorial: Old Kentucky Home
Photo: Larry Tucker

America's Oldest Folk Festival

Bascom Lamar Lunsford learned to play the banjo as a boy growing up in the mountains. Later, when he became a nursery salesman, peddling apple trees to mountain homes, he would take along his banjo, sit and play, and ask his customers if they knew any tunes.

He collected hundreds of old mountain songs that way, and eventually he catalogued thousands, set more than 350 to memory, and recorded many for the Library of Congress and Columbia University. He even wrote a mountain song of his own that became a classic, "Old Mountain Dew."

Although he became a lawyer, he gave up law for his true love, mountain music and dance. He took mountain performers on tours around the country and throughout Europe, even to the White House. In 1928, he founded the Mountain Folk And Dance Festival in Asheville to perpetuate the music he loved. Later, he organized other such festivals including the first National Folk Festival in St. Louis.

He appeared at his original festival every year until his death at 91 in 1973, although he had earlier turned over direction of the event to his son, Lamar. The festival, oldest of its type in the nation, has maintained the integrity Bascom set for it. No gimmicks. Just old-time mountain music and dancing.

"Go natural," he once said of his plan for the festival. "I won't caricature the mountain folks."

The festival is held the first week in August at Asheville's Civic Center on Haywood Street.

BLACK MOUNTAIN

World's Longest Golf Hole

The 17th hole at the Black Mountain Golf Club is 745 yards from tee to green, making it the longest golf hole in the world. It's par 6. The club, on Tomahawk Road, within sight of the beautiful Craggy Gardens of the Blue Ridge Parkway, is open to the public. For more information call (704) 669-2710.

ENKA

America's Champion Weeping Willow

The biggest weeping willow tree in America is in a cove off Sardis Road, next to a spring on Charles and Linda Ford's dairy farm. The willow is 97 feet high with an average limb spread of 108 feet. Its trunk is 7.5 feet in diameter and nearly 24 feet in circumference. Its age is estimated to be 100 years.

OTEEN

World Gee-Haw Whimmy Diddle Competition

Some call it a wooey stick, but to most it is a gee-haw whimmy diddle, perhaps the oldest, simplest and most fascinating of all Appalachian folk toys. Its origins are uncertain, but it dates back at least 200 years, and some believe that Indian medicine men used the toy long before that.

A whimmy diddle is nothing more than a stick with notches cut in one side and a propeller stuck on one end. Rub the notches with another stick and the propeller turns. But there's a trick to it.

The edges of the notches must be rubbed with the finger or thumb as well as with the stick. Rub the left side of the notches with the index finger and the propeller turns right. Rub the right side with the thumb and the propeller reverses. That's where gee and haw, ancient instructions to mules and plow horses, come in. Gee is right. Haw is left.

George Hardy, a retired Defense Department engineer who helped build America's earliest missile-launching facilities, tested whimmy diddles at Wright Patterson Air Force Base and found what makes them work.

"We have to talk about directional damp," he says. "We're converting vertical vibration to orbit through the use of directional damp."

A lot of directional damp is employed on the third Saturday of each May when the Southern Highland Handicraft Guild Folk Art Center on the Blue Ridge Parkway, just north of Asheville, holds its World Whimmy Diddle Contest.

Contestants compete to see who can make a whimmy diddle gee and haw the most times in 12 seconds (16 is the record). Awards are also presented for largest and most unusual whimmy diddles, and many strange and elaborate, multi-propellered whimmy diddles are shown. For more information call (704) 298-7928.

George Hardy demonstrates 4-pronged whimmy diddle

SWANNANOA

America's Largest Southern Crab Apple Tree

The largest Southern crab apple tree in America is 200 feet north of the main gate of the N.C. Department of Human Resources Juvenile Evaluation Center on old U.S. Highway 70. It is 35.5 feet tall with a crown spread of 48.5 feet. The trunk has a circumference of 6.5 feet.

BURKE

MORGANTON

Home of America's Most Famous Witch

Joann Denton, former Sunday school teacher and go-go dancer, first gained national attention in 1976 at age 41 when she was charged under an obscure witchcraft law for accurately predicting a woman's death.

Joann, a diminutive woman who proudly proclaimed her breast size—38—on her car license plate, admitted being a witch, but only a good witch, practicing "white magic." The charge was eventually dropped, but not before she appeared on national TV and was written about in *Time.*

Since then, Joann, who says she first realized she had psychic powers as a small child, has gained more attention by wrongly predicting her mother's death, by staging her own mock funeral, by performing psychic feats at a seance for an *Esquire* writer, by running for mayor of Morganton, and by opening her home, Gray Shadows, as a church.

The house, an ivy-covered stone cottage at 208 Lenoir Road (N.C. Highway 18 north), just three blocks on the same street from the home of former Senator Sam Ervin of Watergate fame, is decorated with such items as a skull and a coffin.

Joann Denton, America's most famous witch (38 bust)

Gray Shadows, home of most famous witch

H. Allen Smith's Totem Pole and Ashes

H. Allen Smith, one of America's most popular humorists, author of more than 40 books, died on a trip to California in 1976, during which he was to appear on Johnny Carson's "Tonight Show." His body was cremated and his ashes shipped by UPS to his home in Alpine, Texas.

Smith had requested no service at his death, so his wife, Nelle, and daughter, Nancy Van Noppen, buried his ashes in the back yard next to an Alaskan totem pole his publishers had given him many years earlier to mark the success of his third book, *Low Man on a Totem Pole*.

His wife dumped a cup of spaghetti and a glass of wine, one of Smith's favorite meals, into the grave, and tossed in a crumpled page from his notebook, which he never went anywhere without.

A short time later, Smith's wife moved to southern Florida, and his daughter had her father's totem pole shipped to her home in Morganton. Three years later, she got to thinking about her father's ashes off in Texas all alone and had them dug up and mailed to her.

For months the small package bearing the ashes sat on her kitchen counter. "I knew that was where my father would love to be sitting," she told her son, Allen, who frequently played with the package without realizing it contained his grandfather and later wrote a story about it all for the *Greensboro Daily News*. "He loved to be in the kitchen."

But in the summer of 1981, the family reburied Smith's ashes in the back yard of the Van Noppen home at 310 Shore Drive, where they are once again guarded by his totem pole.

Site of Frankie Silver's Hanging

Frankie Silver was a jealous woman, and one night near Christmas of 1832, suspicious that her handsome husband, Charlie, had been seeing another woman, she attacked him with an ax while he slept with their two-year-old daughter in his arms in their cabin in a cove along the Toe River.

She chopped his body into small pieces and burned them in the fireplace, then told Charlie's family that he had run off with another woman.

But Charlie's father was suspicious, and after a futile search for his son, he consulted a soothsayer in Tennessee who told him Charlie had been murdered. A search of the cabin turned up bones and greasy ashes in the fireplace. More bones and ashes were found in a hole near the spring. A smudge of blood was found on the cabin door, along with a big circle of blood beneath the floor boards. An old hound sniffed out Charlie's heart buried under the front step.

Frankie was charged with murder and taken to jail in Morganton. She never confessed, but while in jail she wrote a long, mournful song about the episode that was taken as an admission of her guilt.

On June 12, 1833, Frankie was hanged from a gallows on Damon's Hill in east Morganton, becoming the first woman executed in North Carolina. Copies of her song, the "Frankie Silvers Ballad," were sold to the throngs that came to see her hanging. The song, 15 verses long, has endured in the mountains. A later version, which changed Charlie's name to Johnny, became nationally popular more than 100 years after Frankie's death.

The site of the hanging, the highest spot in town, is at the corner of Valdese Avenue and White Street, now occupied by a private home.

VALDESE

America's Largest Waldensian Settlement

Waldensians date back to the 12th century in Italy, where the Protestant group frequently was persecuted by the Catholic Church until it won political and religious freedom in 1848.

A population explosion prompted Waldensians in the Cottian Alps to send a search party to the United States looking for a new place to settle. The party decided on a mountainous 10,000-acre tract in Burke County, and the first 29 settlers arrived in May, 1893. They soon were followed by others.

The plan was to form a commune and pay for the land by operating a sawmill, but they had no experience at that and the plan failed. Waldensians were traditionally farmers, winemakers and stonemasons, and the land was divided and sold to individuals who paid for it by following their own pursuits.

The group, which merged with the Presbyterian Church soon after arrival in this country, founded the town of Valdese and a hosiery mill and commercial Waldensian bakery provided the industry to make the town successful.

Waldensians are now merged with the rest of the population, and their vineyards are gone. But many of the beautiful stone buildings built by the early Waldensians still can be seen, and in the 1950s, the

Waldensian Presbyterian Church opened a small museum to keep the Waldensian heritage alive. The museum has since grown into a building of its own across from the church on Rodoret Street. There may be seen furniture, clothing, farm implements and other items used by the original Waldensian settlers. The museum is open Sundays, 3–5; at other times by appointment. Call the church at (704) 874-2531.

CHEROKEE

ANDREWS

America's Oldest Wagon Train

In 1958, a group of people in Cherokee County decided that the state should build a road up Tellico Mountain to connect with a Tennessee highway leading to Tellico Plains. To draw attention to their plan, the group organized a wagon train to follow the proposed route of the road along Davis Creek, through Hanging Dog and on up the mountain.

The state paid little attention, so the wagon train was organized again the following year, and the year after that, and every year since.

It has grown bigger every year. In recent years, it would include as many as 100 covered wagons drawn by teams of mules, horses and occasionally oxen, plus as many as 500 horseback riders.

The wagon train, carrying its own Porta-johns (don't you bet the pioneers wished they could've had such luxury?), now lasts for a week to ten days and follows back mountain roads and trails to different towns each year. It always culminates with a big parade through some mountain town on July 4th.

Did the road ever get built, you ask?

"We never got it," says Don Ramsey, who has been on every wagon train from the beginning. "But we're still tryin'. We're still a-workin' on it."

For more information call Don at (704) 837-2892, or write N.C. Wagon Train, Inc., Andrews, N.C. 28901.

SUIT

World's Biggest
Ten Commandments, Cross, Testament and Altar

At the turn of this century, a Bible Tract Society member named Ambrose Jessup Tomlinson came out of Indiana to pass out his tracts to the largely illiterate people in the mountains of western North Carolina.

He met a small group of people who wanted to form a new church to find the true way to Christ. Shortly before a meeting of the group to establish the church in 1903, Tomlinson trekked to a nearby mountaintop to pray. There it was revealed to him what kind of church the new one should be.

Such were the beginnings of the Church of God of Prophecy, a church that now numbers more than 300,000 members in this country and 85 others.

Thompson, who became the first general overseer of the church, decided in 1940 that because Jacob in the Old Testament marked the spot where he received his vision of a ladder leading from earth to Heaven, a primary mission of his church would be to mark sacred spots.

The first place he decided to mark was the spot where his own church was formed. The church bought more than 200 acres of land, including the mountain on which Tomlinson had gone to pray for guidance, and named it Fields of the Wood. There Tomlinson planned to create a holy place.

He proposed to begin by creating the world's largest Ten Commandments in concrete letters five feet tall and four feet wide on a mountainside across from where he had prayed. He died in 1943 before he saw his dream realized, but he did see the commandments spelled out on the mountainside in lime.

Since that time, the church has marked significant religious spots in Israel and the Bahamas (the site of Columbus's landing, spreading the Word to the New World), but the primary effort has been at Fields of the Wood.

The Ten Commandments have been completed in white-painted concrete. The world's biggest altar, a concrete structure 80 feet long, has been built on Prayer Mountain, where Tomlinson prayed. On top of Ten Commandments Mountain is the world's largest New Testament, an open concrete Bible 30 feet tall and 50 feet wide with a staircase up the middle to a viewing platform on top that will hold 50 people. Nearby is the world's largest cross, a prone concrete structure 115 feet wide and 150 feet long, lined by the flags of the 86 nations in which the church can be found.

A replica of Christ's tomb may be seen, and an outdoor baptismal pool is used by thousands annually. To be built in the future are a motel and a replica of Noah's Ark that will double as a gift shop, according to the Rev. Ted Carroll, superintendent of the park.

Fields of the Wood is on N.C. Highway 294, 18 miles west of Murphy, near the Tennessee line. It is open daily year around and no admission is charged. Picnic areas are available. For additional information, call (704) 494-7855.

GRAHAM

FONTANA VILLAGE

Tallest Dam in Eastern America

Construction of Fontana Dam, a Tennessee Valley Authority project, began on New Year's Day, 1942, as part of the industrial buildup for World War II. It became the highest dam in eastern America when it was completed in 1944.

The dam, which holds back the Little Tennessee River in a 10,000-acre lake 29 miles long, is 480 feet tall and nearly a half-mile wide. It is 375 feet thick at its base, and three million cubic feet of concrete were required to build it. Fontana Lake, which has become a popular resort and recreation area, has an average depth of 130 feet.

HAYWOOD

MAGGIE VALLEY

Jim Miller's Rattlesnake-Milking Pit

Jim Miller was 9 when his father, a circus animal handler, settled in Maggie Valley and opened a roadside zoo. Jim grew up cleaning cages, handling animals, and when he got old enough, milking rattlesnakes.

"It wasn't asked of me, it was expected," he says. "I look back now and wonder why I ever wanted to put my hand on one of them but it was just something that came naturally."

Jim's father opened a small chain of roadside zoos and eventually moved his family to Texas before his death from cancer at age 45. Jim ran one of his father's zoos in Texas for a while but gave it up to go into the construction business when he was 22. His mother, meanwhile, began selling and closing zoos and by 1977 only the Soco Gardens Zoo in Maggie Valley was left.

Jim, who'd spent many happy childhood hours at the zoo, decided he didn't want it to leave the family, so in 1978 he leased it from his mother and took over the operation. It had been 12 years since he'd handled rattlesnakes and on the second day after he opened the zoo for a new tourist season, a big rattler he picked up to milk for an exhibition squirmed in his grasp and bit him on a finger.

Jim turned out to be allergic to rattlesnake venom and nearly died from the bite. He lost his finger and was warned that he might not survive a second bite.

"The doctor said I should find something else to do," he says. "It just made me more cautious."

Jim went on to become mayor of Maggie Valley, the only known rattlesnake-milking mayor in America, but he wishes he could give up that part of his business. He is working on transforming Soco Gardens into a natural habitat zoo with lots of plants and flowers, but he knows that the big rattlesnake pit by the entrance, gaudily visible from U.S. Highway 19, is what brings in the tourists.

"I seriously believe 50 percent of my business comes in because we are milking rattlesnakes ten times a day," he says.

World Clogging Center and Museum

"The word clogging, as far as we can trace it back, just started being used in 1935 in Chattanooga, Tennessee," says Kyle Edwards. "We always just called it mountain dancing up to that time. You see, here in these mountains you've got a mixture. You've got the Dutch, you've got the German, you've got the Irish, the Indian, the black. What it was was just a cluster of dances and they mingled together. It's the oldest dancing I know that's been created in the United States."

Kyle's family has been involved with mountain dancing for as long as anybody can remember. Back in the '20s, Sam Queen of Maggie Valley, who became known as the grandfather of clogging, formed a dance team and Kyle's mother, Elizabeth, and uncle, Kyle Campbell, danced on the team, which performed in the White House for President Franklin D. Roosevelt and the Queen of England.

Kyle and his wife, Mary Sue, danced on later teams formed by Sam Queen. Their son, Burton, became world champion clogger in 1981 at age 18. Their daughter, Becky, won two United States female clogging championships by age 13. The family organizes dance teams and tours the country with them.

In 1982, Kyle, a road grading contractor, built a huge barnlike building across from his house on U.S. Highway 19 in Maggie Valley. Called the Stomping Ground, the building has a huge dance floor and seating for 2,000 people. Kyle hopes to make it the world center for clogging. Dances and shows are staged nightly from April through November, and he is developing a clogging museum in one section of the building dedicated to his late mother. A fee is charged for shows and dances.

First Southern Ski Resort

Tom Alexander, a guest ranch owner, became the father of Southern skiing when he opened three ski slopes with rope tows on a hillside pasture at his Cataloochee Ranch in 1960.

Tom and his wife, Judy, had started their ranch in 1934 to take vacationers on horseback tours along mountain trails, and they had been looking for something to give them business year-round. Tom made several trips to New England to observe skiing and decided it might go in North Carolina. He built rope tows in his pasture and installed snow-making equipment to insure that he had snow.

The slopes were an immediate success, and in 1968, Tom, who died in 1972, expanded his operation by moving a mile along the same ridge where he cut seven new slopes starting at an altitude of 5,400 feet and dropping to 4,660 feet. On these slopes he build a double chair lift, t-bar lift and rope tows.

Tom's success spawned other ski resorts. Ten now operate in North Carolina's mountains, attracting thousands of skiiers each winter.

Cataloochee Ranch is on Fie Top Road, off U.S. Highway 19, four miles northwest of Maggie Valley. It's open for skiing daily December 1–mid-March.

WAYNESVILLE

America's Oldest Ramp Festival

Outside the Appalachian Mountains, a ramp is generally thought to be an access to a major highway, or a sloping passage connecting different levels of a building, or whatever. To mountain people, ramp means more. Good eating, for one thing. Bad breath, for another.

Ramps are small wild plants that grow in mountain woods. Members of the leek family, they resemble green onions and taste similar to garlic, only stronger, some say.

Mountain people eat ramps raw and cook them with eggs, potatoes, country ham and other dishes, and many look forward to spring when the ramps make their brief appearance.

Back in the '30s, a group of old-timers in Waynesville took to going off to Black Camp Gap, between Maggie Valley and Cherokee, to hunt ramps each spring and cook them into favorite dishes. The group gradually grew as members invited more and more friends to go along. Soon, politicians discovered the group and the possibilities of attracting news media attention by eating the loudly flavored but little-known plants. The event became too unwieldy to hold in the woods and was moved into Waynesville, where it became one of the highlights of the year.

The event is now held the first Sunday in May at the American Legion Park on South Welch Street. American Legionaires, who sponsor it, fan out through the mountains gathering 20 or so bushels of ramps to assure that everybody who wants to taste one has the opportunity.

Dinners of country ham and ramps, barbecued chicken and ramps are sold, and the entertainment includes mountain music and dancing. But the high spot of the day is the ramp-eating contest. Winners have been known to eat as many as 90 raw ramps, and only the people closest to them know how long it takes them to recover.

"The scent will stay with you," says American Legion Adjutant Willard Francis. "You can smell them on a person's breath for four or five days—and it smells terrible."

For more information, call Francis at (704) 456-8691.

Other ramp festivals are held at Barnardsville in Buncombe County and Cherokee in Swain County.

HENDERSON

FLAT ROCK

Carl Sandburg's Final Home

Carl Sandburg, beloved poet, biographer of Lincoln, lecturer and singer of folk songs, was 67 when he and his wife, Paula, came to Flat Rock from Michigan looking for a warmer climate and better pastures for their goats.

They bought 243 acres on Big and Little Glassy Mountains and a 15-room house built for the secretary of the treasury of the Confederacy, and here Sandburg spent his final years.

A late riser, Sandburg took two upstairs rooms on the west side of the house, away from the morning sun, for his bedroom and writing room. It was in this house that he finished his novel, *Remembrance Rock*, and wrote his autobiographical memoir "Always The Young

Strangers." It was in this house, too, in his wife's downstairs bedroom that he died on July 22, 1967, at age 89.

After his death, his wife, who died in 1977, sold the farm, called Connemara, to the National Park Service to be opened to the public. Except for the removal of his basement library to make room for service areas, the house is exactly as it was when Sandburg died. Even the goats and cats in the barn are descendants of Sandburg stock.

The house, on Little River Road, off U.S. Highway 25, is open daily, 9–5, (except Wednesdays, 9–12) at no charge.

HENDERSONVILLE

World's Largest Gravestone
For World's Largest Twins

Until they were 9 years old, Billy and Benny McCrary were much like any other identical twins. But at that age they simultaneously came down with measles so seriously that they had to be hospitalized.

After that, their bodies began to burgeon. Each weighed more than 200 pounds at age 10. At one point they were gaining weight at the rate of 100 pounds a year. Doctors determined that they had pituitary gland problems set off by the measles, but nothing could stop them from gaining weight. In high school, they weighed 400 pounds each and were formidable guards on their school's championship football team.

Shortly after high school, each weighed nearly 500 pounds. Unable to find jobs, they helped their father on his farm near Hendersonville, getting around to their chores on minibikes.

They rode their minibikes in Hendersonville's Apple Festival parade one year and somebody saw them and asked them to appear at two motorcycle shops. On their second appearance, in Greensboro, photographer John Page took a shot of them from the rear on their minibikes that appeared in *Life* magazine and later in the *Guiness Book of World Records*, which proclaimed the brothers the world's largest twins.

From that point, the twins were in show business. They appeared in Las Vegas playing trumpets and telling jokes with a 400-pound go-go dancer. They became a wrestling team and worked up a daredevil routine on their minibikes. They traveled the world.

And all the time they continued to grow. Both topped 800 pounds before diets brought them back to the 700-pound range, where they stayed.

Their size (Billy's waist was 84 inches, Benny's 81) caused them many problems. They drove separate, reinforced and specially equipped cars. Each had to buy two seats in airliners and neither could get into an airliner toilet (Billy once became trapped in one and had to be cut out after an emergency landing). Their own furniture had to be reinforced and they carried small jacks to put under motel beds to keep them from collapsing.

They often spoke of having operations to reduce their size, but the lure of show business proved too great and they continued in it year after year, putting off the operations. Then in the summer of 1979, Billy fell on his minibike in Niagara Falls and injured himself. Complications arose and he died on July 14, weighing more than 700 pounds. His body was returned to Henderson County and buried in the Crab Creek Cemetery, just off Kanuga Road, eight miles west of Hendersonville.

His brother later erected what he says is the world's largest granite gravestone on the grave, leaving one side of it for himself. The monument, 13 feet wide, weighing three tons, features etchings of minibikes in addition to proclaiming the brothers the world's largest twins.

After his brother's death, Benny, who always weighed slightly less than Billy, proclaimed he was going to have surgery to reduce his weight. In 1984, he was still wrestling, still putting on shows, still appearing regularly at the Ripley's Believe It Or Not Museum in Myrtle Beach, S.C., still weighing 700 pounds.

Benny McCrary at grave of brother Billy
World's largest gravestone for world's largest twins
Photo: Buddy Chapman

Original Angel from *Look Homeward Angel*

The marble angel from which Thomas Wolfe drew inspiration for his first and most famous novel, *Look Homeward Angel*, is in Oakdale Cemetery on U.S. Highway 64 west.

Carved by Italian sculptors, the angel stood for years in front of the Asheville monument shop of W. O. Wolfe, Thomas's father. Thomas thought his father was keeping the angel to mark his own grave, but his father sold it, and it now adorns the grave of Margaret Johnson, wife of the Rev. H. F. Johnson, president of Witworth Ferndle College in Brookhaven, Mississippi. Mrs. Johnson died in 1905.

Time has taken its toll on the angel. Both wings, a hand and finger tip have been broken off but replaced and patched. The angel is now protected by a stone wall and high wrought-iron fence.

A bronze replica of the angel has been erected in Asheville's downtown Pack Square, not far from where the original angel stood outside W. O. Wolfe's shop.

Apple Festival

North Carolina is one of the nation's top apple-producing states, and 70 percent of its crop is grown in Henderson County. Credit William Mills for that. He was the first white settler in the area, and he planted the first apple orchard. Now 16,000 of the county's hilly acres produce 7 to 8 million bushels of apples each year, primarily red and golden delicious and Rome beauties, and 32 packing houses ship them to spots all over the nation. Two plants make apple juice.

That gives Hendersonville all the reason it needs to hold a week-long apple festival every year, culminating with the King Apple Parade on Labor Day. The festival, held yearly since 1947, features an arts and crafts show, a quilt show, a gem and mineral show, beauty pageants, clogging and square dancing, mountain music, and contests for the best decorated apples, best apple recipes and best apple window displays.

Original angel from "Look Homeward Angel"

JACKSON

CASHIERS

America's Largest Fraser Fir

In the front yard of the High Hampton Inn, near the 16th hole of the golf course, stands the biggest Fraser fir tree in America. It is 87 feet tall with a crown spread of 52 feet. The trunk has a circumference of nearly 9 feet. Growing beside it, far out of its natural habitat, is a cypress tree.

Highest Cliff East of Rockies

Whiteside Mountain is so named because its southern face is a sheer rock precipice, 1,800 feet high, making it the highest cliff east of the Rockies. The mountain is in Pisgah National Forest, west of Cashiers off U.S. Highway 64 on State Road 1600.

A two-mile hiking trail beginning at a Forest Service parking lot leads to the top of the cliff. Markings on the mountain face are believed to have been made by the expedition of Spanish explorer Hernando De Soto in 1540.

SYLVA

Mystery Rock

Judaculla Rock is 42 feet in circumference, a soft, brownish green stone covered with mysterious symbols, a puzzlement to archaeologists, who believe the symbols were carved by Indians perhaps 1,000 to 3,000 years ago.

The rock is named for a figure from Cherokee legend. Judaculla was born of a virgin princess, fathered by the thunder. He used mountain tops for stepping stones and fired lightning bolts from his bow.

A 100-acre treeless field on the Jackson-Haywood county line bears his name and was thought by Indians to be sacred. According to legend, hunters once tried to enter this field, and Judaculla, angered, leaped after them, stumbled, and caught himself on a big rock.

After disposing of the hunters, he noticed his handprint in the soft stone, then drew a diagonal line across the right corner of the rock and informed all that death would be the penalty for any who crossed the line.

The line and marks that resemble a handprint, along with many other symbols, can be seen on the rock, which is in a 1-acre undeveloped park, the only park in the country with an Indian rock carving as its only attraction.

The park is 9 miles south of Sylva on unpaved Caney Fork Road, 3½ miles off N.C. Highway 107.

MACON

FRANKLIN

World's Rarest Rubies

Late in the last century, a farmer in the Cowee Valley near Franklin found a big red stone on his land and took it to town to try to find out what it was. It was a ruby, and it stirred a sensation.

Tiffany & Co. in New York heard about it and sent a gemstone expert to investigate. In 1893, Dr. George Frederick Knuz made the first official report on the rubies, sapphires and garnets of the Cowee Valley.

Tiffany bought hundreds of acres in the area and dug deep shaft mines along Cowee Creek in 1895. After four years, the company gave up the operation because it was never able to find the source of the stones, which were spread along the creek and the surface of the ground.

Among those stones were pigeon-blood rubies, the rarest and most valuable of all rubies—found in only two places in the world: the Cowee Valley and the Mogock Valley of Burma.

Other commercial operations followed over the years, but all failed to find the source of the stones and folded. Still stones were found by people who lived in the area, or who came to search for them along the creek. People who live in the area tell of finding rubies by the jarful as children and shooting them at birds in slingshots. The late Paul Shuler remembered selling a jarful of rubies for a dollar as a child.

So many outsiders kept coming to the valley looking for precious stones that in 1950, the Gibson family opened a mine to allow tourists to sift buckets of Cowee Creek gravel in search of them. The Holbrooks opened a mine the following year, followed by the Shulers the year after that.

In 1983, 18 mines were operating in and near the valley, attracting thousands of tourists annually. Rubies and star sapphires weighing hundreds of carats have been found by lucky tourists at the mines.

Some mines salt the gravel with cheap, brightly colored foreign stones to mollify tourists who don't find valuable native stones. Others refuse to salt. Among them are Gibson, Holbrook, Shuler, Gregory, Caler Creek, Jacobs, Cherokee and Sheffield. The Cowee Valley is about six miles from Franklin on Cowee Road, off N.C. Highway 28. Most of the mines are open from April through October.

On the last weekend in July, a four-day Gemboree is held at the Macon County Community Building on U.S. Highway 441 South in Franklin. Gemstone dealers and collectors from all over America gather to show, sell and barter their stones.

Inner Tube Races

Tubing has become big sport in western North Carolina. All that's required is a tube from a car or truck tire, or even from a big tractor tire, and a swift flowing stream. Such streams are plentiful in western North Carolina, and if you don't have a tube, many places rent them. It's a lazy sport, tubing. All you do is lie back on your tube and let the stream take you. But even in lazy sports there are always some who are competitive, and that's the reason for the tube races held on the third Saturday each June as part of Franklin's Spring Fling. Races are held for adults and children on the Cullasaja River on U.S. Highway 64 East and Cartoogechaye Creek on U.S. 441 South. For more information call Betty Gideon at (704) 524-3161.

Festival of Festivals

Festivals have sprouted in such numbers in recent years that it's hard for a community to think up an original excuse for having one. So Betty Gideon of the Franklin Chamber of Commerce decided that Franklin should have a Festival of Festivals in 1983, the first such festival in the country. It was such a success that it has been made an annual event the last weekend in June.

This two-day festival offers the best features from 20 different mountain festivals, including such events as clogging, fiddling, Scottish bagpipes, German beer bands and the Cherokee eagle dance. For more information call (704) 524-3161.

HIGHLANDS

Drive-Through Waterfall

Mill Creek falls 120 feet off Rich Mountain to create Bridal Veil Falls on U.S. Highway 64 two miles north of Highlands. The old highway ran under the waterfall and is still open for anybody who has an irrepressible desire to drive through a waterfall.

McDOWELL

JONAS RIDGE

The Brown Mountain Lights

One of North Carolina's oldest and most famous mysteries is the origin of the reddish lights that sporadically glow over Brown Mountain on the Burke and Caldwell county lines. They've been seen since early in the 19th century. Legends have grown around them and songs have been sung about them, but nobody has ever been able to explain them, although many have tried.

The lights have been blamed on everything from UFOs to locomotives. Some attribute them to marsh gas, or foxfire. Others credit atomic radiation, electrical discharges and light refraction from the atmosphere with causing them. Sometimes the lights are just a tinge to the sky, but at other times they seem to move, even to dance, dividing like cells.

They may be seen on clear nights only from a marked overlook on N.C. Highway 181 at Jonas Ridge, or from Wiseman's View in McDowell County, just off N.C. Highway 105, four miles from N.C. Highway 183.

One legend holds that if a dating couple sees the lights, their love was meant to be.

OLD FORT

Imitation Geyser

Andrews Geyser is not, alas, a true geyser. It is more aptly a fountain. Built in 1885 as a scenic attraction to mark the beginning of the long, twisting railroad climb across the mountains to Asheville, the geyser functions by gravity with water piped off a nearby mountain, spraying a constant plume about 60 feet high. It's on Mills Creek Road, off old U.S. Highway 70, northwest of Old Fort.

MITCHELL

BAKERSVILLE

World's Largest
Natural Rhododendron Garden

Roan Mountain, which rises 6,285 feet on the North Carolina-Tennessee line, has more than 600 acres of rhododendron thickets, which turn the mountain pink with blossoms in June, creating a breathtaking natural spectacle of panoramic views from atop the mountain. No other area has such a spread of the common mountain shrubs.

The blossoms peak in mid-June, and on the second weekend in June, the nearby town of Bakersville celebrates the flowering with an annual Rhododendron Festival, featuring a craft show, square dancing, music, beauty pageants and other activities. For more information, call N.C. Rhododendron Festival, (704) 688-3113.

Roan Mountain is on N.C. Highway 261, 13 miles north of Bakersville.

World's largest natural rhododendron garden on Roan Mountain

PENLAND

America's Oldest and Largest Crafts School

Lucy Morgan started the Penland School of Crafts in a single log building in 1923, primarily to teach spinning and weaving to mountain women. The school, first of its kind in the nation, is now America's largest, teaching hundreds of students from all over the world every year in such crafts as weaving, pottery, wood working, metal working, glass blowing, sculpture, jewelry, enameling, lapidary, even plastics.

Eight-week courses are offered in fall and spring and shorter courses in summer. The school now has 33 buildings on 380 hilly acres, and its staff of 70 includes some of the world's finest craftsmen. Many of the faculty members have studios that may be visited, and exhibits of all types are regularly held. The school is northwest of Spruce Pine and may be reached from U.S. Highway 19-E or N.C. Highway 226. For more information call (704) 765-2359.

ALTAPASS

Curviest Railroad Tracks in the East

The Clinchfield Railroad tracks from Marion to Erwin, Tennessee, top the Blue Ridge Mountains at McKinney's Gap near Altapass. In the climb up the mountainside the tracks pass through 18 tunnels in 14 miles.

In order to maintain a grade of less than 1 percent, 18 miles of tracks were used to traverse a distance of only about 3½ miles as the crow flies, as the expression goes in the mountains. At one point, the tracks loop 7 miles to ascend only 300 feet and the loops end only 400 yards from where they began.

It took 4,000 men employing steam shovels, dynamite, mules and oxen three years to build the tracks; 200 of them lost their lives on the job. When the tracks were opened in 1908, they were hailed as the most magnificent feat of railroad engineering in the East.

The Loops, as they are called, can be seen from an overlook on the Blue Ridge Parkway, about two miles north of N.C. Highway 226. From that spot, it is possible to get 14 different views of a train snaking up or down the mountain.

SPRUCE PINE

Minerals Museum

North Carolina is rich in gems and minerals. Rubies, sapphires, emeralds, even diamonds are found in the state. Minerals are found in 49 of the state's 100 counties, and the state leads the nation in feldspar production. The state boasts of more than 300 varieties of gems and minerals.

The Museum of North Carolina Minerals has a study collection of more than 700 catalogued specimens. Exhibits tell about the minerals found in the state, and how they are mined and used commercially. The museum, on the Blue Ridge Parkway at N.C. Highway 226, is open daily, May–November, 9–5; weekends in April.

America's Most Famous Blacksmith Shop

Bea Hensley never knew why he wanted to be a blacksmith, he just always did.

"As far back as I knew how to eat, I knew I could blacksmith," he says. "I was just borned this way."

As a schoolboy, he was able to make whatever he wanted from metal, and he went on to work for an old mountain blacksmith named Daniel Boone before he opened his own shop.

By the time his son, Mike, was a toddler, Ben had him working at the anvil, and father and son came to be a team of master blacksmiths, making beautiful music on the anvil as they worked, creating beautiful objects of metal.

"We do 15th- and 16th-century blacksmithing," says Mike, "beautiful blacksmithing but functional."

That includes andirons, chandeliers, gates, railings and other elaborate decorative items. And the Hensleys do them so well that they have been called upon to do work for Billy Graham's home, for Richard Burton's and Elizabeth Taylor's Hollywood home when they were still together, for Colonial Williamsburg and many other prominent places. Their work is permanently displayed at the Smithsonian Institution in Washington and has been taken on a tour of world capitals.

Foreign visitors come to this country with no other purpose than to seek out the Hensley's small basement shop on N.C. Highway 226 near the Blue Ridge Parkway. Visitors from all over the country stop regularly at the shop to watch them work and hear them make the music of the anvil, something they do every year at the N.C. State Fair.

"I do these things because it's a glory," says Bea, "and money don't enter into it. I like a vision and a challenge. A lot of people chase the rainbow to make money instead of doing what God wanted them to do and they miss the boat."

POLK

LYNN

House Where Sidney Lanier Died

Southern poet, musician and critic Sidney Lanier, best known for his poem "The Marshes of Glynn," died September 7, 1881, at age 39 in a brick cottage at Lynn.

Born in Macon, Georgia, Lanier had roots in North Carolina. His grandfather moved to Georgia from Rockingham County. As a young man, Lanier aspired to be a musician and taught himself to play flute. He became a private in the Confederate Army and saw action in several battles before being captured while serving as a signal officer on a blockade runner out of Wilmington. While in federal prison in Maryland, he contracted tuberculosis, which eventually killed him.

After the war, Lanier walked home, and for the next two years taught school and wrote a war novel. He married and in desperation practiced law for six years before moving to Baltimore where he became flautist for the Peabody Symphony, published his first book of poetry and two books of criticism, and became lecturer at Johns Hopkins University.

Ravaged by his disease, Lanier moved to a tent camp near Asheville in the spring of 1881, hoping to recover his health. In August, he, his wife Mary, and young son Rubin, rented a cottage in Lynn, where they hoped to spend the winter. Lanier died in the cottage sitting before its open bay window watching the sun rise over Howard's Gap. Shortly before his death, Lanier, proclaimed to be the last of the romantic poets, wrote his last poem for his wife:

> So one in heart and thought, I trow,
> That thou might'st press the strings and I might
>   draw the bow
> And both would meet in music sweet,
> Thou and I, I trow.

The house where he died, still a private residence, is on N.C. Highway 108 and is marked with a historic marker in the yard.

America's Finest Collection
Of Prestige Cars

Jim Nelson was a band leader who knew the value of image.

"Show business, I've always said, is at least 90 percent flash," he says. "If you come up in a 16-cylinder Cadillac, they'll give you their money. If you come up in some old scraggly thing, they won't."

That's why Jim, who started out driving a Rolls Royce at 13, always drove only the biggest and best cars. And he rarely got rid of one.

After a crippling heart attack at age 35 in 1952 stopped him from driving, he began collecting big, prestige cars. He now owns 67, appraised by some as the finest such collection in America. He once was offered $500,000 for a single car, he says, and turned it down.

Some of those cars may be seen at the Tryon Antique Car Museum on N.C. Highway 108 at Lynn, just north of Tryon.

Among the cars displayed are the biggest Lincoln, Cadillac and Packard ever made. The Lincoln, a convertible, was built for the movie *Parrish* at a cost of $100,000. The Cadillac is an armored limousine built for President Dwight Eisenhower at a cost of $250,000. The Packard was built in 1939 for Mayor Jimmy Walker of New York. Called the Queen Mary, it weighs five tons and was capable of running more than 200 miles per hour.

Other cars of interest are a 1924 Chrysler Imperial that outraced the Crescent Limited from New York to Charlotte, a 1930 16-cylinder Cadillac that appeared in several Humphrey Bogart movies and a 1908 Brass Ford built and driven by Henry Ford before he opened his first factory.

The museum is open Saturdays and Sundays, 10–6, for a small fee.

Jim Nelson's Other Treasures

After Jim Nelson's heart attack caused him to give up his music career, he became a dealer and collector of fine antiques. His personal collection grew to the point that in 1977 he bought the old Mimosa Inn, built in 1792, reconstructed in 1903, to house it all.

He turned the entire downstairs, including the large dining room, into a private museum. Most of the 12 bedrooms and 12 baths upstairs are packed with antiques as well.

Downstairs is an ornate 1,000-year-old crystal chandelier made to hang in the Doges' Palace in Venice, vases painted by Rembrandt, Louis XIV's bedroom suite, one-of-a-kind porcelain figures of Louis and Marie Antoinette that once belonged to the German emperor, three of the first ten pianos made by Steinway, a Graphophone made by Edison that won grand prize at three international exhibitions, a brass bell from the original Delta Queen, the first vacuum cleaner (a hand-pump model), and hundreds more rare items.

Jim, who is blind, still leads visitors through his collection and tells stories about each item. The collection is shown by appointment only. Call (704) 859-9481.

MILL SPRING

World's Largest Collection
Of Running Edsels

Few other people liked it, but in 1958 when Ford brought out its new pucker-faced car, the Edsel, Willard Jolley loved it.

"When they came out, they were odd and see that's what killed 'em with a lot of people," Willard says. "But I liked 'em because they were odd. They were just odd enough to me to be pretty."

World's largest collection of running Edsels

The Edsel, of course, turned out to be one of the biggest boondoggles in automotive history. Ford made only 110,000 of them and lost hundreds of millions of dollars before stopping production in 1960.

About a third of those cars still exist in one condition or another and Willard Jolley, a retired highway department worker, has more than 40 of them, more in running condition than any other collector.

"I didn't mean when I started for it to come to anything like this," he said. "I was just wanting to get me a '58, a '59 and a '60, make me three nice cars, but I just kept a-buyin' 'em and a-buyin' 'em, and a-buyin' 'em, and I got in real deep here."

Willard displays his cars under sheds in a big field next to his house, about 100 yards off N.C. Highway 108, about a mile west of Mill Spring, and he loves for people to come and look at them at no charge. He calls the place Edsel Acre, and it is marked by the tail fin of a large bomb. That's Willard's little joke. In automotive circles, the Edsel was called the E-Bomb.

TRYON

World's Smallest Daily Newspaper

The Tryon Daily Bulletin, established in 1928, calls itself The World's Smallest Daily Newspaper. It is the size of a standard sheet of typing paper, less than a third the size of most newspapers. Published Monday through Friday, the paper has a circulation of about 3,000.

RUTHERFORD

BOSTIC

Abraham Lincoln's Real Birthplace?

History books say that Abraham Lincoln was born February 12, 1809, near Hodgenville, Kentucky, but a lot of people in Rutherford County believe he was actually born in a log cabin on a steep hill above Puzzle Creek, off an unpaved road near Bostic.

Near the end of the 18th century, an unmarried woman named Lucy Hanks wandered from family to family in Rutherford County doing spinning. In the course of her travels, she acquired two daughters, Mandy and Nancy. Convinced that the children needed more stable upbringings, she placed them in the homes of others when they were 10 or 12. Nancy went to the home of Abraham Enloe, farmer, teacher, community leader.

Shortly after the turn of the century, Enloe moved his family westward and established a farm on the Oconaluftee River (a reproduction of it can be seen at the entrance of the Great Smoky Mountains National Park near Cherokee). Nancy went with them, but unbeknownst to the family, she was pregnant. When her condition began to show, Enloe's wife became upset, thinking her husband the father.

Nancy disappeared from the household, and for months her whereabouts were unknown. She reappeared with a healthy baby boy and Enloe gave Tom Lincoln, an itinerant laborer, a team of horses, a wagon and money to take Nancy to Kentucky and marry her.

Some Rutherford residents believe Nancy returned to the old Enloe cabin in their county to have her baby. After Lincoln became famous, many older county residents signed affidavits saying they'd seen Nancy there with her child.

Who was the child's father? Some believe it was Enloe; others think it was Richard Martin, who courted Nancy briefly in Rutherford.

This is the story told in a 1920 book, *Abraham Lincoln, A North Carolinian With Proof*, by Dr. J. C. Coggins, a Rutherford teacher and legislator.

Tom Melton, a Bostic insurance agent, farmer, and former principal of Bostic School, believes it is true. He has located the remains of the stone cellar of the old Enloe cabin above Puzzle Creek and frequently leads visitors through the woods and undergrowth to see them. He requires each visitor to carry a stone to place atop a pile he has created at the site as a marker. Some day he hopes to have the site preserved and a more suitable marker erected. For more information, call Tom at (704) 245-4731, or (704) 245-0853.

CHIMNEY ROCK

Wash Tub Races

The requirements are simple. It must be a galvanized wash tub; it must have brakes and a steering apparatus, and it must roll without benefit of any power other than gravity.

But there is gravity aplenty on the steep and twisting road from the top of Chimney Rock to the meadows in Chimney Rock Park, and that's the course for the annual wash tub races in mid-August.

Usually, more than a dozen wash tub pilots compete for trophies in two-tub elimination heats.

These aren't the only races at Chimney Rock, a 350-foot stone pillar that got its name because it once was a favorite spot from which Indians sent smoke signals. A sports car hill climb is held the last weekend in April, and hot air balloon races were held for the first time in 1983, although they may not become an annual event.

Visitors to the private park on U.S. Highways 64-74 may ride an elevator in a shaft carved through 258 feet of stone to an observation platform atop Chimney Rock for a stunning view of Lake Lure. For more information, call (704) 625-9611.

FOREST CITY

Charlie Yelton's Bottle Houses

It was 1970. Charlie Yelton had retired after working 50 years as a mill hand, and he was looking for something to do. He'd broken his leg helping a son set up a house trailer, and while he was recovering he saw a feature on TV about somebody out West who'd built a small house out of bottles.

That was it. From then on, he knew what he would do. He would build himself a house with bottles. He started searching in dumps, carrying a burlap sack, gathering castaway bottles. Gradually, they accumulated, bottles of every type, size and color.

He'd never built a house before and didn't know how to go about it, but he laid a brick foundation and started building walls with clear quart bottles, setting the mortar between them by hand. He framed the windows with green 7-Up bottles and created a blue cross under the front eave with Milk of Magnesia bottles.

It took him more than four years and 11,987 bottles to complete the house, and when he finished he filled it with . . . what else? . . . furnishings made of bottles and more unusual bottles.

After the first house, he went on to build two more smaller ones, plus a bottle wishing well and a bottle flower garden.

Thousands of people have come to see the houses, which fill with diffused light by day and often by night.

"It's prettiest when the moon is full and there's no leaves on the trees," Charlie once told a reporter. "It lightens up in there just like daylight."

Charlie's bottle village is behind his house at 937 Cherry Mountain Street. He welcomes visitors. Call him at (704) 245-2094.

Charlie Yelton and bottle houses

Charlie Yelton inside his bottle house

SWAIN

CHEROKEE

Tuffy Truesdell's Wrestling Bears

Tuffy Truesdell was for three years the world's middleweight wrestling champion, but he was dissatisfied.

"I wasn't making any money wrestling, even with the championship," he says. "So I decided I was going to get me a gimmick. I went down South and got me an alligator."

Tuffy went on the road wrestling a 9-foot alligator, more often than not getting the worst of it.

"They were always trying to bite you," he says of the several alligators he wrestled over the years.

They frequently succeeded. He was bitten all over his arms and hands, got a severe gash in his head, had a knee ripped out, even suffered damage to a more personal part of his anatomy.

"Ripped the tail lights right off me," Tuffy says. "Alligators, there's no intelligence. We was on equal terms."

After Tuffy married a Canadian woman, he settled in Canada and opened a roadside zoo and alligator farm. That was where he bought his first black bear, which he named Victor. He and Victor were great pals and they often wrestled for fun. Soon the lure of the road began to tug at Tuffy again.

"I sold the zoo and went on the road with the bear in '62," he recalls.

Tuffy had trained Victor well and landed him several appearances in TV shows and movies. They also toured the country wrestling. But the wear of the road began to get to Tuffy again, and in 1977 he settled in Cherokee and opened a bear-wrestling tent next to the trading post owned by his old wrestling friend Osley Bird Saunooke, former Cherokee chief and heavyweight wrestling champion of the world, on U.S. Highway 441 North.

Tuffy gradually added more bears until he had a couple of dozen and built a series of pits in which to display them. All of the bears have names and many perform. Tuffy and his employees still climb into the pits to wrestle and play with favorite bears, and visitors, who pay a small fee, may purchase vegetables and marshmallows to feed the bears.

The original Victor died in 1978 of a heart attack on a trip to Portland, Maine, in a stationwagon with Tuffy, who gave him mouth-to-mouth resuscitation trying to save him.

"We couldn't even talk about it for a couple of years," Tuffy says of Victor's death. "It was like losing somebody in the family."

Tuffy Truesdell, bear wrestler

World's Largest Bingo Game

Bingo games in North Carolina are limited to churches and charitable organizations and tightly restricted. But the Cherokee Indian Reservation isn't bound by those laws, and in 1982, the tribal council transformed an unused sewing plant into a 4,500-seat bingo hall and opened the world's largest bingo game.

Games are held every other Saturday year-around, and players come by chartered bus from all over eastern America for the regular $300,000 jackpots. In July, 1983, Cherokee Bingo held the first million dollar bingo game, with 4,500 people paying $500 each to play. For more information call (704) 497-2770.

The Oldest and Roughest Sport in America

Long before the first European explorers and settlers set foot in North Carolina, the Cherokee Indians were playing stick ball. It was a ceremonial game, played as part of ancient fire festivals, and it was rough. "The Little War," the Cherokees called it.

It was a simple game. Two teams of lean young men gathered in the center of a field. At two ends of the field were goals made of young saplings. Each player carried a short stick with a cup on the end. A medicine man tossed up a small ball, about the size of a walnut.

After that, it was a free-for-all. The goal was to get the ball through the other team's goal by whatever means. The only rules were that the ball had to be lifted from the ground with sticks, and the sticks couldn't be used as clubs. Anything else was allowed—kicking, tripping, flailing, wrestling, boxing, hair-pulling, scratching, biting.

The game continued until one team attained a set number of points. Old-timers tell of games lasting two days and of players being carried off the field with broken bones and bloodied faces.

The game was highly popular on the Cherokee Reservation early in this century. Each community on the reservation fielded a team and took fierce pride in it. Betting of livestock, firearms and knives was common at games.

High school football has replaced stick ball for the Cherokees, but the old game is still played once each year during the Cherokee Fall Festival on the second weekend in October. The stick ball game usually is held on Saturday afternoon on the high school football field. For more information call (704) 497-9023.

America's Most-visited National Park

The Great Smoky Mountains National Park, 514,093 acres of wilderness, lies astride the North Carolina–Tennessee line and contains some of the highest peaks in eastern America. It attracts more visitors than any other national park, most of whom drive through on U.S. Highway 441, the single highway through the park, connecting the popular resorts of Cherokee and Gatlinburg, Tennessee. In summer, traffic sometimes backs up for miles along the highway as tourists stop to gawk at black bears that frequently gather at the roadside to beg handouts.

Terminus of America's
Most Beautiful Highway

If there is a more beautiful highway anywhere than the Blue Ridge Parkway, it would be hard to imagine. The 469-mile scenic highway runs from the Shenandoah Valley in Virginia to the Great Smoky Mountains National Park in North Carolina, following the crest of several mountain ranges at an average elevation of 3,000 feet.

Begun in 1936, the highway is complete except for a 7.7-mile stretch around North Carolina's Grandfather Mountain scheduled for opening in 1987. The highway has no commercial traffic, no stop signs, no stop lights and no billboards. It does have numerous overlooks, exhibits, visitor centers, museums, hiking trails, picnic areas and camping sites. The highway, which runs for 250 miles in North Carolina, has its western terminus on U.S. Highway 441, just north of Cherokee.

Living Cherokee Village

When the first European settlers arrived in North Carolina, the Cherokee Indians, a large and powerful tribe, controlled western North Carolina and parts of Virginia, Tennessee, South Carolina, Georgia and Alabama. A proud and civilized people, they lived in villages and farmed.

But as settlers moved steadily westward, many battles were fought and the Cherokees gradually lost their lands. Still, early in the last century, Cherokees controlled great areas and some had built prosperous plantations and owned black slaves.

In 1820, the Cherokees instituted a constitutional republic, modeled on the U.S. Constitution, and in 1821, a Cherokee named

Sequoyah introduced a Cherokee alphabet and a Cherokee literature was begun.

In 1828, however, gold was discovered on Cherokee lands, and settlers began pressuring the government to force the Cherokees off. In 1838, 7,000 federal troops rounded up 14,000 Cherokees and marched them to the Indian Territories of the West, now Oklahoma. More than 4,000 Cherokees died on the way, and the march became known as "The Trail of Tears."

But about 1,000 Cherokees managed to avoid the troops and hid out in the Great Smoky Mountains. They gradually emerged and eventually got back 56,000 acres of the more than 7 million they had lost. This land became the reservation of the Eastern Band of Cherokee Indians, which now numbers more than 8,000 members, nearly 6,000 of them on the reservation.

The Cherokee heritage is preserved at the Museum of the Cherokee Indian on U.S. Highway 441 North, which houses the largest and finest collection of Cherokee relics in eastern America, along with the largest collection of writings by and about the Cherokees. Displays and a movie tell Cherokee history and legends.

Adjoining the museum is the Oconaluftee Indian Village, where

1750 cabin in Living Cherokee Village

visitors can see a reproduction of a Cherokee village with demonstrations of Cherokee life before the arrival of settlers.

Unto These Hills, an outdoor drama about the Cherokees, is presented nightly in summer at the nearby Mountainside Theater.

The museum is open Monday–Saturday, 9–8, and Sunday, 9–5:30, in summer months; daily, 9–5:30, the rest of the year. Oconaluftee Village is open 9–5:30, mid-May through October.

Making dugout canoe in Living Cherokee Village

TRANSYLVANIA

PISGAH FOREST

America's First National Forest And Forestry School

Gifford Pinchot, America's first trained forester, began the first scientific forest management in America in 1892 on lands owned by millionaire George Vanderbilt, who was building a mansion near Asheville. Pinchot was succeeded by German forest master, Carl A. Schenck, who started America's first school of forestry, the Biltmore Forest School, in an area called the Pink Beds in 1898.

In 1911, Congress authorized the purchase of lands in the area for Pisgah Forest, the first national forest, and after George Vanderbilt's death in 1915, his widow gave vast acreage to the government to become part of the forest.

The campus of the Biltmore Forest School has been reconstructed using seven of its original buildings and opened as an exhibit at a museum called the Cradle of Forestry in America. Exhibits of early forestry and a movie may be seen at the visitor center, open daily. The museum is on U.S. Highway 276, five miles south of the Blue Ridge Parkway. The forest offers many camping and recreational areas.

The Original Waterslide

Waterslides are fairly recent developments in the amusement business, but this waterslide has been in use probably for hundreds of years. Indians are believed to have been the first people to have fun sliding down Sliding Rock.

Looking Glass Creek spreads to a thin sheet as it courses 60 feet over the broad slick rock into a clear pool eight feet deep.

The rock has been a popular recreation site for decades, and even Lassie, the famous movie dog, once slid down it for a scene in a TV show.

Original waterslide

Photo: Clay Nolen

The rock is smooth enough to slide on without a mat, but a double-layered swimsuit is advisable for tender rumps. The U.S. Forestry Service has built bathhouses and a parking area at the top of the falls, which is on U.S. Highway 276, eight miles north of N.C. Highway 280.

SAPPHIRE

Highest Waterfall in Eastern America

The Whitewater River drops more than 411 feet in two levels over the side of Round Mountain to create Whitewater Falls, the highest waterfall in eastern America, more than 200 feet higher (but considerably narrower) than famed Niagara Falls. The waterfall is on an unpaved road 10 miles off U.S. Highway 64 near the South Carolina line. A sign on U.S. 64 directs the way.

WATAUGA

BLOWING ROCK

South's First Theme Amusement Park

The East Tennessee and Western North Carolina Railroad, a narrow-gauge line between Boone and Johnson City, Tennessee, opened the northwestern mountains to development at the end of the last century. The railroad's small steam engines ran over the longest narrow-gauge track in the country and became affectionately known as "Tweetsie"

Highest waterfall in Eastern America
Photo: Clay Nolen

because of their shrill whistles. Floods that washed out the tracks in 1940 brought the railroad's end.

In 1957, Grover Robbins, a local businessman, bought the line's engine No. 12, built three miles of track for it on a hillside on U.S. Highways 221–321 between Blowing Rock and Boone, and opened it as the South's first theme amusement park.

Tweetsie Railroad is open daily from Memorial Day to Labor Day and weekends in September and October.

Tweetsie R.R., South's first theme amusement park

WILKES

WILKESBORO

Jail Where Tom Dooley Was Held

There are those who still maintain that Tom Dula didn't do it, that he gallantly went to the gallows to protect his one-time lover, Ann Foster Melton.

Tom and Ann grew up together along Reedy Branch in Happy Valley near the Wilkes-Caldwell county line and were lovers by the time Ann was 14. But Tom went away to fight in the Civil War, and in his absence, Ann, a beautiful young woman, married James Melton.

But Tom, a handsome lad, did return, and he and Ann picked up their relationship where they left off, although Ann remained with her husband. Meanwhile, Tom also started a relationship with Laura Foster, Ann's first cousin.

Several months after his return from the war, Laura disappeared and was found dead in a shallow grave on a ridge, stabbed through the heart. Tom fled to Tennessee after Laura's disappearance but was arrested and returned to the Wilkes County jail, where he was held until her body was found.

Many believed it was Ann who killed Laura after she discovered Tom was planning to leave with her.

At his trial, Tom was defended by the flamboyant lawyer Zeb Vance, a popular former governor, and the trial was given front-page coverage by the *New York Herald*. Tom was convicted largely by circumstantial evidence and hanged before a crowd of 3,000 on May 1, 1868.

John Foster West, a mountain writer who thoroughly researched the story for a book, *The Ballad of Tom Dula*, found it to be more a sordid tale than a romantic one.

Tom, he says, was a mean, low-life sort, feared by many who knew him. He was suspected of killing a man in Wilmington during the war who discovered him having an affair with his wife. West believes the motive for Laura's murder was syphilis. Tom, Laura, Ann, James and

Pauline Foster, who lived with Ann and played a role in the case, all were infected with the deadly disease for which there was then no cure. West believes Laura was killed because she gave the disease to Tom, who then spread it to the others.

But the romantic version of the story prevails, largely because more than half a dozen ballads were written about the case. One of them, "The Legend of Tom Dooley," became an international hit for the Kingston Trio in 1959.

The Old Wilkes Jail, built in 1859, where Tom was held, is now a free museum, open Monday–Friday, 9–5; Saturday by appointment. The museum is at 103 N. Bridge Street. For more information, call (919) 667-3712.

YANCEY

BURNSVILLE

Lumberjack (and Jill) Day

Trees are big in Yancey County. Pisgah National Forest makes up 40 percent of the county's land area, and timbering is the major industry. Lumberjacks abound, and they look forward to the day each October when they can prove whose skills are best.

Competitions are numerous. They include log loading and stacking, felling trees in precise areas, chopping trees with double-edged axes, and sawing trees with bow saws, two-man crosscut saws and chainsaws. Since lumberjacking is no longer a one-sex trade, lumberjills compete in some contests.

The day-long event is held on the third Saturday in October each year at East Yancey Middle School, two miles east of Burnsville on U.S. Highway 19-E. For more information, call Bob Cleary of the U.S. Forestry Service at (704) 675-9959.

MT. MITCHELL

Highest Point in Eastern America

The peak of Mt. Mitchell, 6,684 feet above sea level, is the highest in eastern America. Once called Black Dome, the mountain was first measured by Dr. Elisha Mitchell, a University of North Carolina professor, in 1835.

After his measurements were challenged in 1855 by Congressman Thomas Clingman, Mitchell returned to the mountain in 1857 to verify his findings and fell to his death over a 40-foot waterfall. He is buried on the summit of the mountain, which was named for him after his death.

In 1915, the state bought 1,224 acres of Mt. Mitchell and made it North Carolina's first state park. The summit can be reached on N.C. Highway 128 off the Blue Ridge Parkway. A tower at the top provides a beautiful panoramic view.